The SIZZLING HISTORY of
Miami Cuisine
CORTADITOS, STONE CRABS & EMPANADAS

MANDY BACA

AMERICAN PALATE

Published by American Palate
A Division of The History Press
Charleston, SC 29403
www.historypress.net

Copyright © 2013 by Mandy Baca
All rights reserved

All photographs courtesy of the author unless otherwise noted.

First published 2013

Manufactured in the United States

ISBN 978.1.60949.901.3

Library of Congress CIP data applied for.

CONTENTS

Introduction   5

1. The Ingredients   11
2. Why Miami?   21
3. Pre-Columbian South Florida—Early Miami   29
4. 1920s–1940s   47
5. 1950s–1970s   67
6. 1980s and Beyond   81
7. Dairies, Supermarkets, Fast-food Restaurants and a Bakery   99
8. Recipes and Other Finds   107

Conclusion   127
Endnotes   131
Bibliography   135
Index   157
About the Author   159

INTRODUCTION

But the bright side is that Miami's optimism, coupled with its unique geography, has, over the course of its one-hundred-plus years, made it like nowhere else in America…or rather North America.[1]*—Scott P. Cunningham*

Miami is a world all its own, and as poignantly mentioned above, like no other place in the country. Ask anyone what he or she thinks of Miami, and the following is conjured up:

"Southern American (politically liberal, anti-big government) with strong Latino influence (and a lot of ultra-conservative Cuban ex-pats)."

"When I think of Miami, I think Latin American culture predominated by Cubans and mixed with a healthy elderly Jewish population."

"Alligators, crazy people, sex, beach, Cubans and Europeans, tourists."

Ask anyone what constitutes Miami's cuisine, and you'll hear the following:

"The only thing I can come up with is rice, fish and lots of fruits, like pineapple. Also, there's a lot of beef consumption."

"Miami cuisine equals Cuban plus other Latin American influences mixed with basic American."

"Cuban with some Jewish items mixed in."

A lot of the above is true, but other parts feed into the negative stereotype that is often associated with Miami. Incorporated on July 28, 1896, Miami is a city that was created from the dreams of our forefathers from the cold North, who were looking for new land, new vacations and, most importantly, new dreams. They were looking for a new Naples, one could say, and if at the very least, a new Jersey Shore, which at the time of Miami's incorporation was considered America's playground. In contrast to other cities that came to be out of necessity, Miami was created for the enjoyment of others. Why else would the early settlers willingly move to a fly-infested swamp that was, at the time, more isolated and dangerous than Perth, Australia? While Miami was incorporated in 1896, much later than the rest of the country, the area has a long and rich history of wars and diverse settlers, making it one of the earliest inhabited locations in what is considered the New World. Findings of pre-Columbian settlements in the area have been traced as far back as ten thousand years ago.

To dispel the preconceived stereotype, Miami is no longer just sun, sand and party. It is most recently an epicenter for fashion, arts and culture. Food-wise, Miami has flourished in the past thirty years, and world-renowned chefs and innovative cuisine have made it a permanent fixture on the world's food map. It is now an important hub and a top contender when comparing the best food cities in America.

But how did we get here? And why do we eat the way we eat? There are hundreds of books about the history of Miami and hundreds of Miami and/or Florida cookbooks, but none that merge the two as a conclusive history of Miami's cuisine.

A popular quote amongst food lovers is that of separating those who eat to live from those who live to eat. For those that eat to live, it's easy to write off food as nothing more than sustenance and the occasional form of entertainment—a necessary part of society and human interaction. It's also easy to forget that food is an evolutionary being that is not stagnant. Food history is important because it teaches us about a specific community and its evolution. In this case, Miami, a magic land for newcomers and the land of the transient, food is especially important, as it acts as a form of identity and helps with assimilation. It also provides an exceptional view of the progression of a city—its highs and lows—as well as its people.

A lot of history can read like a timeline, filled with dates and not very entertaining. In researching and reading history, the mundane always seems to take a backseat, and little details of the daily lives of common society were rarely recorded. In the present day, with the likes of Facebook, Twitter and Instagram, all of the intricacies and the banality of life are being recorded and will be forever stored in the realms of the Internet so that when the twentysomethings of this generation grow up, they can have a detailed view of what their life was like back in the 2000s. In the same fashion, I want this document to read like a story—the story of Miami through the lens of food and a compilation of the food stories throughout the centuries told by the people who lived them. To kick it off, here are a few stories from one of HistoryMiami's projects, Make Miami History Now, which is aimed at saving Miami's memories:

Shrimp cocktails on Key Biscayne at the Hurricane Harbor Lounge were $1.50, and Leonard's La Pena on Bird Road served ONLY shrimp cocktail and steak. Whitey graciously showed you to your table at The Pub on Coral Way, where the lettuce wedge was huge. Sam & Carl's Deli on Red Road was a favorite, too, serving a "Messy Bessy Sandwich." A trip into Coral Gables netted you delicious pastry at Andalusia Bakery, and there was Woolworths and Jan's for outrageous ice cream concoctions. Jimmy's Hurricane on Bird Road, Chesapeake Oyster House in the Gables, and Perrine were popular restaurants.[2]—Molle Grad

My one grandmother would take us to Junior's on 79th Street and Biscayne Boulevard, where they had great breads and rolls. My other grandparents used to take us to the Roney Pub for dinner. We loved that big quarter-wedge of iceberg lettuce they'd give you with a choice of dressing. We'd also go to Corky's for pastrami and corned beef back in the days when I ate big, meaty sandwiches. Corky's used to have a drive-up area where you could order from your car window, and they'd bring your food out to your car and hook a tray to your car window.[3]—Jody Collins

I worked as a hostess at Maisel's Restaurant, then known as Junior's, on the corner of 79th Street and Biscayne Boulevard. Having come from up north, I could not believe that the restrooms and water fountains were segregated; "White" and "Colored" signs were placed on them. This restaurant, like Wolfie's, was very popular. We used to have long lines.[4]—Heike Greenwood

One thing I remember is that there were numerous delicatessens in Miami as I was growing up. You had The Stage Deli, Wolfie's, Junior's, Rascal House, The Famous Deli, Rubendales, Gold Start, and Corky's to name a few. Each one served delicious and large corned beef sandwiches and kosher dill pickles. Where have they all gone? Once a week, my family would eat at the Coral Way Cafeteria, which later became the Biscayne Cafeteria, on Miracle Mile near Ponce de Leon Blvd. (I continued that tradition with my husband, three children and even with my grandchildren until the cafeteria finally closed.) For special dinners (maybe once or twice a year), we ate at the Ember's Restaurant on the beach or the Pub on Coral Way. Of course, you can't forget the Studio Restaurant on 32 Avenue off of Coral Way. I can still taste their special garlic bread and onion soup to this day. The Miami Springs Villas had a special restaurant that served prime rib that was second to none. When we were young and would go out on dates, we had so many wonderful places to go, and like all kids do, we would go in large groups like a swarm of bees. Red Diamond Inn had to be one of our favorites on Le Jeune Road. Their pizza was the best. On Miracle Mile, we would go to Jahn's Ice Cream and get the "kitchen sink." (Back then, I guess we weren't as germ conscious as we are now.) Then, of course, how can I forget the hot glazed Krispy Kreme donuts when the bakery was on Tamiami Trail? It is amazing how easy it was to eat a dozen hot donuts then. A favorite any time of the day was Royal Castle. For those who never experienced Royal Castle, you really missed a treat. Small hamburgers, grilled with onions while you were there, served on a nice fresh roll with the best birch beer in an ice-cold mug.[5]—Loretta Barish Morris

Having lived in Palmetto Bay for over 30 years, I have many memories, such as dining at Black Caesar's Forge on the corner of 152 Street and 67 Avenue, famous for their potatoes baked in a tree resin. We also had land crabs the size of a small dinner plate running through our yard. It was impossible to drive 152 Street without running over them. I never see any large ones anymore; once in a while, a few small ones appear.[6]—Annita DeWitt Middleton

Miami in the Miami Vice eighties was glamorous, fast-paced, and a little scary. Still, I enjoyed going to clubs such as Cats, Suzanne's, The Mutiny, and Faces in the Grove. One night, while at Biscayne Babies, my sisters and I even met Senator Ted Kennedy.[7]—Gina Lee Rice Guilford

On Miami Beach, [I remember] *eating at Pickin' Chicken, Picciolo's Italian Restaurant, Wolfie's—on 21st Street and on Lincoln Road, The Noshery at the Saxony Hotel, Famous Restaurant on Washington Avenue, and Hoffman's Cafeteria on Collins.*[8]*—Michael Pearlman*

The study of history is an exhaustive one, and I hope to open your eyes to the beauty of that which is Miami's food history. I am here to provide you with the starting ingredient in the hopes that the study of our local traditions will be upheld and preserved. At the very least, I hope you'll have learned something unique about Miami that you didn't already know.

Chapter 1

THE INGREDIENTS

NATIVE VERSUS NONNATIVE

Miami is a cornucopia of products and flavors. I know you've heard that one before, but here's a closer look at what that exactly means. Did you know that Florida fishermen catch more than 84 percent of the nation's supply of grouper, pompano, mullet, stone crab, pink shrimp, spiny lobsters and Spanish mackerel?[9] Another fun fact is that avocados were once originally called alligator pears because of their rough, hard, green exterior. Lastly, after California, Florida is the largest producer of edible food in the country. Before its incorporation, Miami was extremely rural, and when it came to food, it was all about the ingredients and how to procure them; there were no talks about restaurants, chefs or unique organic farms. There were only a few paved roads, the areas were heavily overgrown and there was a large concentration of wildlife. Charles Featherly, an important early figure for the preservation of farming initiatives and food memories, conducted an extensive farming census of all Dade County's endeavors. He found the following to be the most prominent and important crops to be grown: tomatoes, beans, grapefruit, oranges, pineapple, apples, peppers, eggplant, mangos, guavas, avocados and lemons.

That shouldn't be a surprise to many, as Miami rests at the heel of the Florida peninsula and is surrounded by Biscayne Bay on one side and the Everglades on the other, offering bountiful soil and access to many products.

W.C. Smith on his pineapple plantation. *Courtesy of the State Archives of Florida, Florida Memory Project.*

Seminole Indians harpooned manatees for food. *Courtesy of the State Archives of Florida, Florida Memory Project.*

But before we get into that, let's take a trip through time and take a peek at the life of the first inhabitants of the area, the Tequesta Indians, who settled at the mouth of the Miami River where it meets Biscayne Bay. What remains of their past is preserved at the location of present-day Miami Circle in the heart of downtown Miami. The history books detail what these first settlers enjoyed (while some of these delicacies exist today, others have disappeared in use and popularity through the passage of time): saw palmetto, berries, cocoplums, gopher apples, pigeon plums, sea grapes, palm nuts, prickly pear fruit, cabbage palm, hog plum, turtle meat and turtle eggs, deer, terrapin, a variety of fish, lobster, trunkfish, snails, whale, venison, squirrel and turkey. They also ate clams, oysters and conchs, but shellfish was a minor part of the diet. The sea cow (manatee) and the Caribbean monk seal were delicacies and reserved for the important leaders of the tribe. All this dramatically changes after civilization moves in.

One cannot talk about Miami food without tackling the topic of the ingredients. What's native? What's nonnative? What's the difference? The orange is eponymous to Florida, so it's native, right? I'll admit that I was confused at first, too. As Raymond A. Sokolov notes:

> *Before the Columbian Exchange, there were no oranges in Florida, no bananas in Ecuador, no paprika in Hungary, no tomatoes in Italy, no potatoes in Ireland, no coffee in Colombia, no pineapples in Hawaii, no rubber trees in Africa, no cattle in Texas, no donkeys in Mexico, no chili peppers in Thailand or India, and no chocolate in Switzerland.*[10]

In order to fully understand the study and/or history of food, one must define what types of foods these ancient people feasted on in detail. One must also define the types of products that were already available and/or native and differentiate them from the types of products that were brought over and naturalized. What makes a plant native anyway? There is much confusion and debate as to what is truly from the area and what is not. There is a lot of wrong information in books, many of which simply use the incorrect wording. There are many books that detail what grows best in a certain region, but most fail to detail the origin of these foods, and just because it can be grown in a region does not mean that it is indigenous to a said region. A lot of the food products that are native to the area are things that we would not use nowadays. In a *Tequesta* article from 1942 titled "Food Plants of the DeSoto Expedition," the first example of what is considered the original American diet from 1500 is detailed: Chicasaw plums; wild sweet potato; sunflower seeds; acorns; Jerusalem artichoke; persimmons; plums; honey locust seed pods; chestnuts, which they would use for oil and bread; hickory nuts; corn; calabash gourds; mulberries; strawberries; blackberries; sassafras; young onions; pumpkins; beans; yaupon; wild peppers; and coontie.

"Miami is located in what is considered the lowland humid tropics. This means a lot of different things. This area is rich in productive starchy perennial staples. Crops like bananas, breadfruit, sago palm, peach palm, air potato, and Tahitian chestnut are very high yielding. The region is also well supplied with perennial oilseeds like oil palms, Brazil nuts, and avocados. In the study of plants in pre-Columbian times, it has been shown that what was going on in Florida varied greatly from that of other southern states. Florida sites lacked many of the starchy plants and contained different species of nuts as compared to more northern locations."[11]

There are over fifty edible plants native to the area, including American licorice; American persimmon; clovers; California walnut; Dillen's prickly pear; cow parsnip; Lisban yam; Darling plum; gopher apple; ground nut; pigeon pea; pond apple; sea grape; saw palmetto; tabasco pepper; yerba buena; red maple, which is used in the production of maple syrup; cocoplum; Seminole pumpkin; strangler fig; Indian fig; pokeberry; cabbage palm; and the muscadine grape. In the early days of Florida, the most important plants were the guava, cabbage palmetto, pineapple, yucca, lime, sapodilla, coontie and the Seminole pumpkin. Fish and other seafood native to the area included alligator, blue crab, clams, flounder, grouper, king mackerel, mahi-mahi, mullet, mullet roe, oysters, pompano, red and yellowtail snapper, shrimp, Spanish mackerel, spiny lobster, stone-crab claws, swordfish, tilapia, tilefish and yellowfin tuna. Slow Food International is an organization on a mission to preserve food traditions and food products. A variety of local products that are in danger of extinction include the Wilson Popenoe avocado, American persimmon, Hatcher mango, Pantin mamey sapote, Florida Cracker cattle, Gallberry honey, traditional sourghum syrup, sea grape, Royal Red shrimp and the Hua Moa banana. All of the products are part of Slow Food International's Ark Food preservation project.

Regardless of whether or not a product is native or nonnative, what can be grown in the greater Miami area? All of the aforementioned native crops can be grown, along with the following: bananas; blackberries; blueberries; cantaloupes; coconuts; papayas; pomegranates; basil; chives; cilantro; cumin; oregano; parsley; rosemary; sage; thyme; mint; corn;

hearts of palm; shallots; pecans; white mushrooms; peppers (green, red, yellow, orange, habanero, banana, finger hot, jalapeno, red chili, sweet, hot); mamey sapote; lychee; passion fruit; tangerines; tamarind; guarapo; saoco; ugli fruit; calamondin; mirliton (chayote); atemoya; black sapote; canistel; jackfruit; loquat; jaboticaba; longan; *monstera deliciosa*; *muntingia calabura*; white sapote; sugar apple; annatto (achiote); boniato; dasheen (taro); malanga; yam; plantains; snap beans; pole beans; lima beans; beets; broccoli; cabbage; cantaloupe; carrots; cauliflower; celery; Chinese cabbage; collards; sweet corn; cucumbers; eggplant; endive-escarole; kohlrabi; lettuce (crisp, butterhead, leaf, romaine); mustard; okra; onions (bulbing, green); peas; Southern peas; potatoes; sweet potatoes; radishes; spinach; summer spinach; squash (summer, winter); strawberries; turnips; watermelons (large seedless, small); Brussels sprouts; cassava; dandelion; dasheen; dill; fennel; garbanzo beans; garlic; kale; leek; luffa gourds; honeydew melons; rutabagas; blood oranges; pomelos; sour oranges; tangelos; carambola (starfruit); dragon fruit; kumquats; Tahitian and Persian limes; wax jambu; and peanuts.

The following is a list of the fish and other seafood that can be caught in Miami's waters: amberjack; catfish; dolphin; grouper; Florida pompano; flounder; mullet; mangrove snapper; red snapper; bay scallops; blue crab; clams; conch; Florida spiny lobster; mussels; oysters; shrimp (pink, brown, white, rock, stone); five types of tuna; wahoo; cobia; and kingfish.

As the Florida Food Guide notes:

The first inhabitants of Florida included various tribes of Native Americans who were hunters and fishermen. These indigenous people relied on Florida's wildlife as their major source of food. The Florida natives hunted bison, deer, and other animals and foraged for wild nuts and berries. With the arrival of Ponce de Leon from Spain in 1513, the multicultural infusion of Florida's food began, signaling a drastic change in diet for Florida natives. As more European explorers came to Florida, the state's culinary styles became extremely diverse. Not long after the Spanish began to settle in Florida, more immigrants began to arrive, including the Africans who were brought to America as slaves during the 16th century. The foods and dishes of the Native Americans, Spanish, and other Europeans were greatly influenced by the ingredients, spices, and methods of food preparation that the Africans brought from their home country. White Americans who migrated south to settle in Florida also played a major role in flavoring the taste of Florida's regional cuisine. They found various ways to use

A day's catch of fish in the Everglades. *Courtesy of the State Archives of Florida, Florida Memory Project.*

Florida's indigenous ingredients like guavas, fresh seafood, wild ginger, and many more local foods. As time progressed, the basic Spanish and Southern cuisine of Florida blended with that of a number of other cultures.[12]

Christopher Columbus played a crucial role in the transference of food information, as his arrival set in motion a trail of very important events, including European diseases that wiped out millions of indigenous people, invaded with armies, killed armies of people and uprooted cultures. Columbus introduced Old World crops to the New World and vice versa. Sokolov writes:

Everyone speaks an idiolect—his own personal language that functions within the larger speech community. A full-blown dialect is a set of idiolects so similar they form a recognizable minilanguage: the Spanglish of United States Chicanos, the nasal twang of the Great Lakes, Valley Girl talk in California. The same thing happens in the kitchen. Every family has its own set of recipes and eating habits, its idiocuisine formed by foods being passed down from the previous generation and through contacts with new foods, flavors, and tastes. And if the similar experiences of many neighboring families evolve into a new "dialect" of eating and cooking— because these families have all changed their idiocuisines after galvanizing

16

contact with new conditions, ingredients, and food ideas—then the world has a new regional cuisine.

Cuisines evolve almost instantly when two cultures and their ingredients meet in the kitchen, and old cuisines never die; they add new dishes and ingredients to old recipes and slough off the losers, the evolutionary dead ends. The net quantity of culinary diversity probably remains the same, and of course we now take cooking seriously enough to write down recipes for the dishes that are in danger of disappearing.

This process of constant evolution in the world's kitchens went into high gear 500 years ago when Columbus landed in the West Indies. By 1600, Europe and the Americas had exchanged the fundamental ingredients and ideas of their cuisines.[13]

Gary Ross Morimo adds:

Like sugarcane, the orange made a journey to the New World that was long and legendary. First mentioned in the Five Classics of Confucian China, the orange migrated from Asia to Malaysia, and then to India, Persia, Africa, Sicily, and southern Spain. In the garden of earthly delights, the orange held an honored spot. Columbus introduced citrus to the star-crossed Spanish colony at La Navidad, and Dominicans and conquistadors carried seeds across the Straits of Florida. A dazzling variety of oranges took root in Florida.[14]

Today, the study and preservation of our native products are kept alive in the research centers of The Kampong, Fruit and Spice Park and the Fairchild Tropical Botanic Garden. Additionally, The Kampong was the historic site of the Jelly Factory, owned by Captain Albion Simmons, who planted guavas and made jelly and wine from them. This eventually became the home of David Fairchild, who had the task of introducing many tropical plants (approximately thirty thousand) in the area and the rest of the United States.

guava wine ??

SASSAFRAS JELLY

Ingredients:
6 roots of red sassafras
3 cups water
1 bottle of liquid pectin
3 cups wild honey
*3 tbsp sassafras powder

Preparation:
Wash the red sassafras roots and boil in the 3 cups of water until water is reduced to 2 cups. Strain liquid into another pot an add one bottle of liquid pectin (used for making jellies.) Bring to simmer. Add the honey and sassafras powder. Simmer 10 minutes. Pour into clean, hot preserve jars. Cover, cool and store.*

Note:
sassafras powder: remove bark from the sassafras roots and dry, then grate or pound into powder.

Recipe taken from the *Florida Heritage Cookbook* (1976), by Marina Polvay and Marilyn Fellman.

LIONFISH

More recently, the high danger of the lionfish, a nonnative predator/invasive species, has risen in obtrusiveness. There is a large campaign in the area to rid the waters of this disruptive fish—so much so that the government has stepped in and declared that you don't even need a license to fish them. The first sightings of this fish in the Miami area date back to the early 1990s. Why are they invasive? They eat native fish and eliminate organisms, which are important to the reef system of the local area. They also compete for food along with native fish such as grouper and snapper. They are similar to snapper in taste and in how they are prepared. Eat more lionfish.

COONTIE

Coontie (*Zamia floridana*) is also known as arrowroot and resembles a small fern or palm. A native primitive plant, the coontie was an important source of food in the times of early South Florida. At one point, it became the single most important source of income for settlers of the frontier town. The plant itself is poisonous, but through a process of grinding the root and turning it into a paste that is then fermented and used as flour, it becomes fit for consumption. The coontie was especially popular with the Seminoles, who arrived in Florida in the 1700s.

Early settlers to South Florida would also find use in the crop, as it was an important source of food in an area that sometimes did not have the necessary basics, and it sold well in the market of Key West, prompting a boom of several factories in the 1840s. The Seminoles taught the early settlers the many uses of the plant.

Between 1848 and 1849, the Ferguson brothers operated a small coontie mill on the Miami River off of present-day Thirty-second Avenue, using waterpower to grind the tough root. They operated as one of the more successful coontie mills, employing twenty-five people and grossing sales of $25,000 from shipments to Key West. But they were gone by the 1850s.

The crop eventually died out with the real estate boom of the 1940s into the wooded areas of western South Florida. It could not be domesticated, and runoff water from the washing of the arrowroots proved dangerous to the residents of Miami. Grits replaced coontie.

The coontie plant was also extremely diverse in its uses. One of the area's oldest cookbooks, *The Florida Tropical Cook Book*, offers a variety of uses for the home. The plant can still be found growing wildly in many parts of the city, even while traipsing through downtown Miami. In the modern day, the coontie plant is planted to attract the Atala butterfly.

SUGGESTIONS AND RULES FOR USING FLORIDA ARROWROOT STARCH

1. *It makes an easily digested food for those of delicate digestion.*
2. *Children are especially fond of the various desserts made from this wholesome starch.*
3. *Do not fail to make griddlecakes with it, using one-third Florida arrowroot starch instead of that much flour.*
4. *You will find not flat, raw taste when using Florida arrowroot starch in creamed codfish toast and other recipes where milk is used.*
5. *In puddings, pies, sauces, etc., if not enough Florida arrowroot starch is issued, the result will be thin or stringy. Add a little more starch, and cook again.*
6. *In ice cream custards, this starch excels others. Try it and see how creamy it makes the ice cream. Allow one tablespoonful to a quart.*

7. *For a burn, try this. Mix in a very little water a teaspoonful of Florida arrowroot starch and then pour on a boiling water to make it jelly; when cool enough, apply to the burn.*

8. *In all gravies, sauces, etc., this starch will never fail to bring success if the right proportion is used.*

9. *When you wish to make fruit jellies or transparent desserts, nothing is so nice as Florida arrowroot starch.*

10. *It is especially nice for laundering all the delicate fabrics. Use it once and you will be well pleased with your results.*

11. *Use the juice of lemons in clear starch puddings or desserts. It improves the flavor.*

ARROWROOT DROP CAKES:

Cream one-half cup of sugar with one-half cup of butter, beat separately three eggs, stir beaten yolks into butter and sugar, also a level cup of Florida arrowroot starch in which a teaspoonful of baking powder has been mixed; last, add white of eggs little by little; flavor with grated rind of lemon, fill tins half full. Bake moderately to a light brown.

From *Biscayne Bights and Breezes: A Cookbook with Loving Memories of Miami* (1987).

Chapter 2

WHY MIAMI?

The all-important question persists: Why Miami? We know why the early settlers arrived, but what about the emigrants after incorporation? The answer is very simple: location, location, location. Miami sits in a very interesting location, serving as the true gateway to the Americas in either direction. Miami's proximity to the islands of the Caribbean and Latin American countries and similar weather makes for an easier transition. And in many cases, many of these immigrants already had experience with Miami, in both business and leisure. In Latin American countries, Miami is considered the Mecca for shopping. I've heard countless stories of how past relatives would arrive to Miami with long lists ready to shop at the downtown stores of Burdine's, Jordan Marsh and, later, Dadeland. The coming of the Cubans helped ease the transition for future groups to emigrate as well. Thinking about it psychologically, people frequently dislike change and, when faced with new environments, stick with the known. In this case, people of Latin American descent will generally stick with other Latin American groups. The arrival of the Cubans paved the way for a better life in the United States and set an example for future groups to come.

Miami-Dade County is commonly referred to as Miami. It gets confusing for newcomers and outsiders not living in Miami. Miami-Dade County is made up of cities, villages, towns and neighborhoods of varying sizes, some no larger than a mere two city blocks. The city of Miami is included in the county. In terms of this book, I will refer to Miami-Dade County as Miami, as that is the local norm. When applicable, I will refer to a specific section by its appropriate name. The best way to explain it would be to compare it to a borough. Miami is made up of more than a dozen boroughs, each with unique characteristics. This stems from the beginnings of Miami, during the 1920s land boom, when everyone came to create their own little community to become the king of their own real estate domain—to partake in the piece of the very large puzzle. This spirit has been a guiding force and is still present today. Like any large city, each borough also has its own food identity. I will define what each borough is known for food-wise but will steer away from detailing specific restaurants, as this is not a dining guide. In some instances, I will provide more detail about a specific restaurant, but only as it may provide depth to the text or to highlight historic restaurants. Miami is a city that likes to destroy itself. Preservation is still a new concept in Miami, and it heavily applies to restaurants, too. Food preservation is important, and if a restaurant has withstood the test of time, it is something to take note of—especially in Miami, where the concept of the latest trend supersedes the authentic or historic. Most recently, the idea of restaurant empires and longstanding eateries are becoming the norm, but that general thought is relatively rare in Miami.

Nationally, Philadelphia has the Philly cheesesteak, Rhode Island has coffee milk and Chicago has deep-dish pizza. Internationally, Genoa has pesto, Parma has prosciutto and Melbourne has Vegemite. But in Miami, where influences come from many parts of the world and varying customs, it is not accurate to deem the croquette or Cuban coffee as the cuisine signifier for the city. Miami is not just Cuban. True, there is a large Cuban population, and much of the city's flourishing occurred because of this group, but for that, you might as well just go to Cuba. A complete understanding and/or explanation of Miami's cuisine requires a look through time and a visit to many establishments of varying ethnicities, customs, traditions and history. From the very beginning, there's been a strong cultural mix from all over the world, and it has changed greatly throughout the years—in a sense, remaking itself again and again—due to both internal and external factors. Its beginnings were with the adventurer and the immigrant. It's geographic location has played a large role in its changing evolution, serving as the gateway into the Americas while combining both the local flavors of Miami, taking inspiration from native local ingredients, and the different cultures that have brought their own foods, ingredients and flavors.

What is cuisine? Cuisine is the cooking practices and traditions that are influenced by external forces, local ingredients, history and culture. Cuisine is affected by everything from religion, nutrition and agriculture to economics,

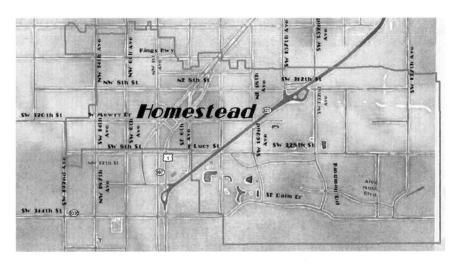

Map of Homestead. *Credit: Phillip Ulbrich. Sources: GEBCO, NOAA, National Geographic, DeLorme and Esri.*

politics and psychology. It also tells the story of immigration, amalgamation and assimilation through the language of food.

Miami-Dade County can be divided into four main sections: Southwest, Central, North and the beaches. The following is a listing of Miami's different cities, towns, villages and neighborhoods and their most prominent demographics. While demographics are not the only definitive markers for the types of food that are present and/or prevalent in a specific area, the following is a good measurement for Miami. Groups are listed by order of influencing number.

Southwest Miami-Dade County

Homestead: Mexican, Caribbean
Redland: Mexican
Cutler Bay aka Cutler Ridge: American, African American, Trinidadian
Kendall: Nicaraguan, Cuban, Peruvian, Venezuelan, Colombian, French
Westchester: Cuban, Argentine, Uruguayan, Venezuelan, Colombian, Dominican, Puerto Rican, Nicaraguan, Salvadoran, American
Sweetwater/Fontainebleau aka Little Managua: Nicaraguan, and to a lesser extent, Cuban, Colombian, Honduran
Doral aka Little Venezuela and Little Bogota: Venezuelan, Colombian

Central Miami-Dade

Little Havana: Central American, Cuban
Downtown Miami: Central American
Wynwood aka Little San Juan: Puerto Rican
Overtown: African American
Little Haiti: Haitian
Allapattah: African American, Dominican
Liberty City: African American, American
Coconut Grove: Jamaican, Bahamian, Barbadian, African American
Coral Gables: Peruvian, Cuban, Venezuelan, Colombian

North Miami-Dade

Hialeah: all Central and South American, specifically Cuban, Dominican, Honduran, Nicaraguan, Columbian
Opa-Locka: African American
North Miami: Asian, Brazilian, Haitian
Aventura: Asian, Jewish, Brazilian
El Portal: Jamaican, African American
Miami Gardens: Jamaican, African American, Bahamian, British West Indian, Colombian, Cuban, Haitian, Dominican, Nicaraguan

The Beaches

Key Biscayne: South American, Brazilian
South Beach: Jewish, European, Cuban, Brazilian, Peruvian, Venezuelan
Mid-Beach aka Little Tel-Aviv: Jewish, Argentine
North Beach: Italian, Argentine, Uruguayan, Jamaican
Surfside: Jewish, Brazilian
Bal Harbour: Jewish
Sunny Isles aka Little Moscow: Asian, Jewish, Brazilian, Russian, Ukranian, Belorusian, Lithuanian, Latvian, Moldavian, Uzbek, Chechen
Bay Harbor Islands aka Little Brazil: Brazilian

Throughout its history, Miami has experienced a series of different immigrant patterns—periods and/or significant markers that have changed the entire demographics and landscape of an area. This is highly due to the transient nature of the area. First, we had the Tequesta, who ruled the land

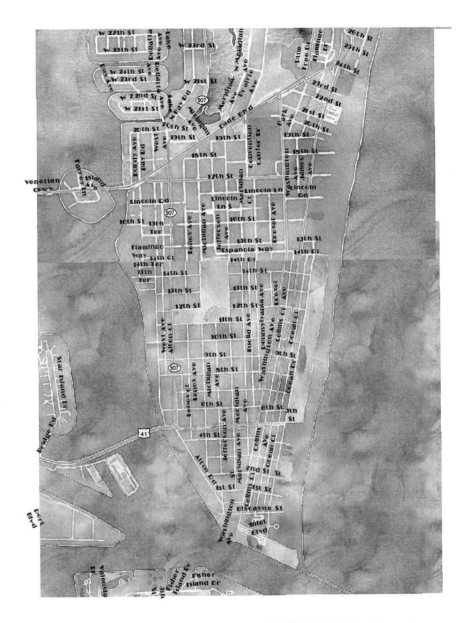

Map of South Beach. *Credit: Phillip Ulbrich. Sources: GEBCO, NOAA, National Geographic, DeLorme and Esri.*

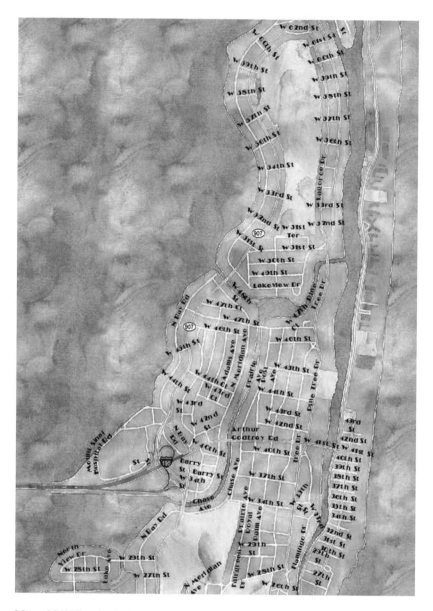

Map of Mid Beach. *Credit: Phillip Ulbrich. Sources: GEBCO, NOAA, National Geographic, DeLorme and Esri.*

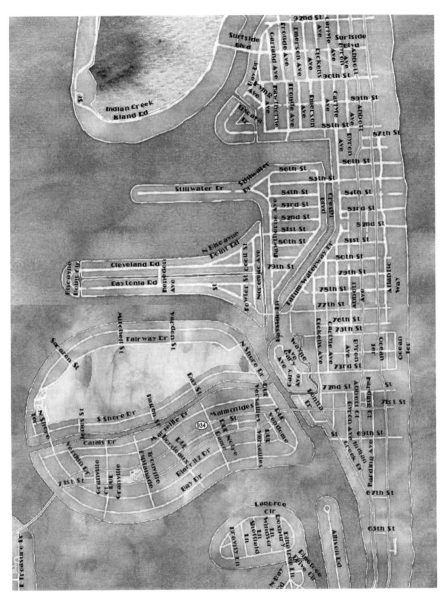

Map of North Beach. *Credit: Phillip Ulbrich. Sources: GEBCO, NOAA, National Geographic, DeLorme and Esri.*

for ten thousand years. The tribes became extinct by the 1800s due to their interactions with the many new settlers. Bahamians began emigrating to South Florida and the Keys in the 1800s. But more and more, white settlers from the East Coast of the United States began settling into the area in the late 1800s, pushing out the Bahamians. Miami then became entirely southern, white and Jewish and stayed like this well into the late 1950s. The Cuban Revolution of 1960 prompted two large waves of immigration into Miami, pushing out the Jewish community and moving into their neighborhoods. In the 1980s, instability in Haiti spurred another wave of immigration that coincided with the third wave of Cubans and people from other Latin American countries who were fearful of their own unstable governments and looking to experience the American Dream. With each new group came new foods, new traditions, new customs, new experiences—all of which contributed to the vibrant melting pot that is Miami.

The above are the main influences that continually change Miami. There is, of course, a smaller population of European, Middle Eastern and Indian settlers, but they do not impact in the same numbers as the aforementioned ethnic segments. We are diverse in the Asian and Latin American ethnicities but not in much else, and that has been a large criticism for Miami. Many of these other groups have moved and found their homes in the cities of Broward and Palm Beach. Every community has a section specifically known for something. In Miami, it is the same. But at the same time, Miami is an evolutionary city, and it will change, especially with the changing demographics of certain enclaves and the expansion of areas. Brickell is now encroaching on Little Havana, and there is a large population of young professionals and families of varying backgrounds moving into the areas of Edgewater and Buena Vista on the border of Little Haiti.

Food is a great teacher; there is no greater marker of the passing of time and the tastes of people than food. Look at Miami and the changes that have occurred. They're prevalent not only in restaurants but also in cookbooks and in the home. Ethnic groups that come bring their flavors, ingredients, recipes and traditions and try to recreate it here, but it is always different. Over the years, assimilation in food can be seen in the houses of Miamians, where lasagna is served with tostones (fried plantains) instead of garlic bread, and children have learned to eat foods not normally found in their homes, including legim (Haitian vegetable stew). You may even adopt new dishes as your own. On Twitter, the best example of Miami's diaspora was tweeted on March 29, 2013, at 11:00 p.m. by Ed (@LAX2MIA) to @bluecollarmiami: "You're a man of many talents—cook latkes like a bubbe, tostones like an abuela and now fish like a Catholic on Good Friday."

Chapter 3

Pre-Columbian South Florida—Early Miami

Miami Through Incorporation

It's difficult to imagine daily life in the era before colonization—swamplands, no air conditioning and bugs the size of tennis balls. Before air conditioning became mainstream, early settlers would light smudge pots under their dining-room tables to keep the mosquitoes away, as they kept their doors and windows open to fend off the heat. While the area may not have been ideal for living, it is clear that it was conducive to the growing and livelihood of a large number of food products, including the tropical and exotic varieties. A further look into history shows just how important one food product can be. The big freezes in the winter of 1894 set a chain of events that forever changed the area that would one day be called Miami.

Thanks to the findings of local archaeologist Robert Carr, the earliest known evidence of settlement in the area dates back to ten thousand years ago. Carr's findings show evidence of boar hunting in the area of present-day Deering Estate, along with artifacts of ancient food-related tools such as prehistoric toothpicks and bowls made out of shells. It is believed that these people were the Tequesta Indians, the most prominent Native American tribe in Miami, who resided mainly at the mouth of the Miami River. Later, this Native American tribe would also share space with the Seminole Indians, who were the first people to catch and consume stone crabs as we know them today. These early settlements practiced more nomadic customs such as fishing, hunting and

Above: The Everglades. *Courtesy of Justin Namon.*

Left: Old map of Miami.

The Everglades. *Courtesy of Justin Namon.*

gathering, as opposed to agriculture. Even when contact with settlers and conquistadors occurred, they would still not adopt the custom of agriculture. This is one of the big impacts that led to the Tequesta's demise, along with war and introduction of new diseases. Luckily, the area was conducive to a hunter/ gatherer lifestyle, and they lived for centuries and rarely went hungry. Through the course of time, these tribes thoroughly understood the land and seasonality of products. The area of South Florida is the only area in the country that resembles a subtropical nature, more closely related to its neighbors of the south. Even trekking four hours north, travelers can feel the difference. This point is especially important in the growing and cultivation of one of the state's major food products, the orange. "So interesting is the climate in this region, that it is one of the few places where such diverse animals, flora and fauna meet…alligators and crocodiles exist harmoniously along with hawks, bobcats, white-tailed deer, loggerhead turtles and roseate spoonbills."[15]

One of the first groups to make contact with the Tequesta was the Spanish. Pedro Menendez de Aviles and his men visited the Tequesta settlement in 1566 and built a mission at the mouth of the river the following year. The 1700s saw the beginning of pioneers trickling into the area. Numerous Seminole Wars broke out over the course of the 1800s, making the area dangerous and extremely volatile, but new settlers—from other parts of the United States and the Bahamas—continued to trickle into South Florida. By this time, the Seminoles were the main tribe in South Florida, as the Tequesta had died out by the early 1800s.

In 1819, after years of fighting, Spain ceded Florida to the United States, although the cession did not become official until 1821. Once the wars ended, the remaining pioneers became friendly with the Seminole Indians, and the two cultures learned new things from each other. Fort Dallas was built in 1836 on the plantation of Richard Fitzpatrick, which grew astronomical quantities of maize, sugarcane, a variety of tropical fruit and bananas. Fitzpatrick's land is important because it was one of the first large-production farms in the area. Before the coming of Henry Flagler and Julia Tuttle, settlers were unsuccessful in setting up permanent roots in Miami. In 1846, William English took over his uncle's (Fitzpatrick) land along the Miami River and created the Village of Miami—unfortunately, he was fifty years too early. He was onto something though. The area was still too barren and isolated from the rest of the world. He lived on the land that would eventually be sold to Julia Tuttle, where the present-day Hyatt hotel is located.

Due to its geographical location, Florida was part of the Old South, and its economy was dominated by agriculture and subsistence farming as a means to support large plantations. Also being part of the South, Florida was a slave state, seceding from the Union in January 1861. During the Civil War, Florida's most significant wartime role was in providing food supply to the Confederacy, as South Florida became a prime source for beef and salt. But it was not restricted to just food; clothing, iron, guns and swords were also collected and sent to the troops. During this time, Florida, still vastly embodied by the swamp in the south and loosely populated in the north, was a popular refuge for people fleeing the Confederacy. With no direct roads and being accessible only by boat, South Florida became the most isolated and remote area in the eastern United States. While the area was insignificant in terms of population, there was a small fight for the area in terms of water patrolling. Union forces eventually took hold of Biscayne Bay and stopped boats coming from Key West transporting food. This led to further isolation, and the area's residents had to subsist on food from the land. This return to the land is a recurring and common theme in Miami's history and will again be seen in other decades of trouble. The end of the Civil War in 1865 catapulted the era of the homesteader boom.

By the 1870s, there was a significant population in the area, but what were people doing during this time? What were the economic endeavors? Salvaging ships, farming, fishing and hunting wild boar and venison were the top trades of the day. Author Helen Muir notes:

> *While not the first city to be incorporated, Coconut Grove was the first village to be established in Miami around 1825, when it was mainly inhabited by Americans from the North, British and white Bahamian immigrants. At this time, Coconut Grove was more of an extension of the Bahamas, as many of the settlers spent their time going back and forth, most of the time bringing back non-native products with them like soursops, sugar apples, Barbados cherries.*[16]

The area's first true settlement was of black Bahamians in Coconut Grove, and its first permanent resident was Bahamian Temple Pent. Both black and white Bahamians settled in the Coconut Grove area, and the peak of their influence was between 1870 and 1890. Being from the islands and familiar with tropical living, they were essential in teaching newcomers from the North (with the exception of the aforementioned Temple Pent, whose efforts in homesteading the area were unsuccessful) the lay of the land and how to survive. They were beach-living folk, and that was ideal, as there were no paved roads at the time. The Bahamians introduced such delicacies as conch fritters and conch chowder. Black Bahamians introduced pigeon peas, soursop, star apple, sugar apple, Jamaica apples, caneps, sapotes and dillies. The oldest black settlement in the area of Coconut Grove can be found on Charles Street. White Bahamians introduced yams, cassava, eddys, pounders and benne (sesame).

Ralph Munroe's zest for the area convinced the Charles Peacock family to build a hotel on the site of today's Peacock Park. The hotel opened as Bayview House in 1882 and was the first hotel built in the Miami area. A few years later, the Peacock family constructed additional buildings and renamed it the Peacock Inn. The Peacock Inn was the southernmost hotel in the continental United States for a considerable time after.

Both from Ohio and with dreams of finding the holy real estate land, William B. Brickell and E.T. Sturtevant traveled together by yacht to Miami with supplies and building materials in tow. They arrived in the area at the mouth of the river, where the Tequesta once lived, and took up residence on either side, Brickell to the south (a total of 640 acres through the Perrine Grant) and Sturtevant to the north. Along the way, the friends had a falling out with each other. The Brickells set up a trading post and made good business trading with the Seminoles, who offered animal skins, dried fish, beeswax, honey, bear oil, egret plumes and coontie in exchange for clothes, guns, rum, metals, ornaments and cash.

Muir notes:

> *What was it like feeding a family before the railroad? Well, it wasn't easy if one is thinking in terms of supermarkets and lavish selections of food from every part of the globe. But it wasn't that hard, either, if one happened to be tuned to the land and the sea and to sharing and helping one another. In Miami, U.S.A., I wrote about these things and how the women coped. They learned to use guava syrups as the principal sweetening for pies and cakes. They made johnnycake...sweet and plenty of it, stewed venison, ash-baked sweet potatoes, roast hog, gypsy stew (usually made from wild hog, turtle or manatee), coontie pudding and coontie pancakes. Their children never saw milk but they ate Indian sofkee for gruel and boiled Seminole squash, reef bean soup, turtle fry and fried chicken. Most families had a few chickens, but they paid the price by fighting off coons, wildcats, and possums. If they planted vegetables, the deer and rabbits became their enemies. What with wild duck and quail in the hammocks, there was always plenty to eat. The women made good use of fruits like the hog plum, coco plum, sea grape and custard apple, as well as sapodillas, guavas, limes and few pomegranates. The schooner from Key West, which every six weeks picked up the coontie starch, also brought groceries so that the operation amounted to barter. A man could get along fine without ever seeing cash. In earlier days, soap was normally made with leftover beef and pork fat. However, the South Florida settler found excess animal fat in short supply. The problem was solved when it was discovered that nearly a half a year's supply of soap could be made from the clear white fat of just one large alligator.* [17]

Two sequential freezes led all roads to Miami. The first freeze, in December 1894, and the second, on February 7, 1895, hit the entire state of Florida with the exception of Miami. It not only hurt the citrus but also the tomato and pineapple crops. To get an idea of the extent of the freeze damage, the year before the freeze, Florida groves had an estimated yield of 5,550,376 boxes; the year after the big freeze, only 150,000 boxes were shipped. Julia Tuttle immediately sent a package of orange blossoms to Henry Flagler to show proof of the unharmed crops down south. Tuttle's grove survived and flourished, and her oranges were the only ones to be sold in the market that year. But Florida rebounded after the freezes, and the orange is now the state fruit.

After the freezes, Tuttle offered Flagler an offer he couldn't refuse. "Bring your railroad to Miami," she said, "and I will give you half my land." William Brickell offered Flagler some of his land as well. Flagler agreed, and the Florida East Coast Railroad chugged into Miami on April 15, 1896. With the railroad came many new things, including the importation of food that was not readily available or even been known to exist in the area. That year, hoards of southern families, along with their grits, ham, biscuits and collard greens, invaded Miami. And over the next few years, the cuisine remained very primitive and southern in nature.

LEMON CITY AND ALLAPATTAH: THE FORGOTTEN CITIES

Coconut Grove was not the only settlement in the early days of Miami. Lemon City, now more commonly known as Little Haiti, was considered Miami's first agricultural hub, as the small farming community of the 1890s set up vast luscious farms consisting of lemon groves, lime trees, guava trees and sugar-apple trees. Geoffrey Tomb notes, "Lemon City was the largest community on the Southeast Florida mainland in 1895, and now, 101 years later, there's no trace. It's been obliterated. A year before Miami's incorporation, the 1895 population of Lemon City was 300."[18] Buena Vista, located just outside of Lemon City, was also active in the growing of tomatoes. After the arrival of white settlers, black Bahamians were pushed out of Coconut Grove and moved into the areas of Lemon City, Cutler and Perrine.

Allapattah (the Seminole word for "alligator"), now mainly a warehouse and industrial neighborhood in Miami, was also once an important agricultural hub with many dairies and traditional farms. The land boom of the 1920s did not change the neighborhood as dramatically as the rest of the city, and it continued to thrive quietly until the 1960s, when a major hurricane destroyed most of the area and forced many to move elsewhere. During this time, a true melting pot emerged, as it became a popular area for residents looking for affordable housing in close proximity to the downtown area. Yankees, Jews, Latin Americans and Asians from a variety of countries and Italians all lived alongside each other. One of Allapattah's first restaurants was the aptly named Regent Emporium, located next to the Regent Theatre. Unfortunately, it was destroyed by the Hurricane of 1926. The placement of I-95 in western parts of downtown Miami led to a displacement of many black Americans from the nearby neighborhood of Overtown into Allapattah. Today, the area's residents are a mix of black Americans, Dominicans (Allapattah is sometimes referred to as "Little Dominican Republic" because of its high Dominican population), Hondurans, Haitians, Cubans and Nicaraguans, along with other Latin American residents of varying countries. Currently, the neighborhood's largest contributor is The Produce Market, which is Miami's largest open-air food distribution center.

THE BEGINNINGS OF MIAMI

Miami was incorporated on June 28, 1896, in a room over the pool hall on the city's first street, Avenue D. Miami was a instant boomtown, and everyone wanted a piece of the pie. People came from all over the country to see the glorious city, but it wasn't for everyone. Shocked by its roughness, many travelers left immediately, but thankfully, others, the important ones that would help to build the city, stayed. The biggest question of the era was: Can you endure the wilderness? In the beginning of incorporated Miami, the city was mostly inhabited by the populations of the Northeast. People came to Miami for many reasons, including health, money, new opportunities and sun. Nationally, the whole-hearted American diet—i.e. meat and potatoes—was the norm, and the new settlers brought this tradition with them. As Miami was a young city at that point, eating out was not yet custom. Overall, it was not popular, and meals were eaten at home with food that was also grown at home or procured locally. Small two-seat lunch counters existed, but they were only open for two hours during lunchtime. There are few records of these lunch counters. If the occasion permitted an eating outing, these meals were usually eaten at the hotel restaurants, which were extremely popular at the time, as they were grand, luxurious dining halls, some able to accommodate eight hundred people at a time. One of these hotel restaurants was located inside of the White Palace Hotel, which opened in 1911. That restaurant's seating capacity was more than two hundred, and back when the concept of farm to table was nonexistent, this restaurant touted that they made everything from scratch and grew their own vegetables on a five-acre lot that the hotel owned outside of the city. A year later, the *Miami News* proclaimed it as one of the best restaurants in town. Another one of downtown Miami's oldest restaurants was the Boat Restaurant. Luncheons were twenty-five cents, while seafood dinners, which included good coffee, were fifty-five cents. Another plus was that the restaurant was air-conditioned.

Two of the most important food settlers to the area were John Seybold and Jerry Galatis. German-born John Seybold opened his famous lunch counter Seybold's in the heart of downtown Miami on Flagler Street. He eventually expanded the lunch counter to include an ice cream parlor, bakery and candy store. In the 1920s, there was a large anti-German movement, and while his business was prosperous, he was constantly harassed and accused of crimes. People even believed that he was poisoning his bread with tiny pieces of glass. In 1925, he sold his company to Southern Baking Company, but the building in downtown Miami bearing the Seybold name still stands today as an important reminder of Miami's early days. Galatis opened his famous restaurant, The Seven Seas Restaurant and Marine Cocktail Lounge, on what is today the site of Ocean Bank on the corner of SE First Street and Second Avenue in 1913. The restaurant's fresh, upscale seafood and proximity to the theater made it extremely popular, and it stayed open until the 1950s. Lunches rounded out at $0.65, and dinners were $1.25. Galatis had come to Miami from New York but was originally an immigrant from Greece. At this time, Greeks were prominent in the Miami area, many taking up residence in the neighborhoods of Lower Wynwood and the Roads. (They would later leave the area for other parts of Florida, although there are still pockets of the ethnic group in Miami, mostly in the suburbs.) Galatis was an innovative restaurateur and brought the first flashing restaurant sign and marquee to the area. His restaurant also served a number of famous folks, including Amelia Earhart and Al Capone.

Despite its idealistic beginnings, Miami was not without its problems. The city's battle with crime began early. Julia Tuttle's only request for the incorporation of Miami was that it be a dry city. Local entrepreneurs quickly resurrected North Miami, a shantytown with opium dens and saloons open around the clock. Racial conflicts were also a popular theme in Miami's early days. In 1896, Henry Flagler and Julia Tuttle designated a district for Miami's black residents called "Colored Town." Located between NW Sixth and

Exterior of the Seybold Building, which previously housed John Seybold's many food shops. *Courtesy of Aurelia Vasquez.*

Twelfth Streets, it would later be known as Overtown. By 1915, most of the city's five thousand blacks lived in this community, and a color line was drawn in 1911 along certain streets throughout Miami. The city's white residents wished to restrict the expansion of areas inhabited by blacks.

Immediately following incorporation, Julia Tuttle set out to open the Hotel Miami, but the opening of Flagler's grand hotel, the Royal Palm, overshadowed her endeavors. The Hotel Miami was not nearly as popular as the Royal Palm Hotel because it was a dry hotel, and nothing could compare to Flagler's grand, majestic gem located on Biscayne Bay. John Sewell, one of the area's prominent early residents, was appointed by Flagler to clear the land for the hotel in 1896. The building of the hotel saw a quick turnaround, and the grand 450-room hotel with wraparound verandas opened for business on January 17, 1897. All of the top members of society had reservations for the opening dinner—they came from all over the country, and some even came from abroad. The grand dining room had seating for five hundred and on the opening dinner served the following menu: green turtle soup, escalop du Pompano a la Normandie, filet du bouef a la avaur, sweetbread glace

Royal Palm Hotel. *Courtesy of the State Archives of Florida, Florida Memory Project.*

Dining room of the Royal Palm Hotel. *Courtesy of the State Archives of Florida, Florida Memory Project.*

with asparagus tips, quail sur canapes, ribs of beef, claret jelly and tutti-frutti ice cream. The hotel was demolished in 1930 and sat on what is now to be the new Whole Foods in downtown Miami.

Another grand hotel of the time was the iconic McAllister Hotel. Built in 1917, the McAllister held importance in the Miami skyline for many reasons. The tallest building in Miami until 1925, it was considered the city's first skyscraper at ten stories tall and set a boom for the construction of Miami's high-rise buildings. The owner was a wealthy widow named Emma Cornelia Hatchett McAllister, an interesting point, as it was uncommon for women to own and operate businesses of this size at the time. In a 1987 *Miami Herald*, Geoffrey Tomb detailed the comical but serious problem of the high volume of disappearing hotel towels, which were being stolen by the handful to be used as cushioning for bootlegging operations. Sitting on prime location on Biscayne Boulevard and Flagler Street, the McAllister Hotel was sadly demolished in 1989 to make room for new downtown developments.

At the onset of World War I, Miami was used as a base camp for military training. Times were tough if you owned or operated a restaurant during the war. Prices of sugar were exorbitantly high in 1914—so much that one restaurant man complained that his customers were stealing it from him. In 1917, the government instituted Meatless Tuesdays and Wheatless Wednesdays to assist with national food rationing, with the following local restaurants and hotels signing the policy: Green Tree Inn, Wayside Inn, Seminole Café, Davis' Café, Rector Café, National Café, New Haven Café, Belmont Café and Seybold's. As with any law passed at this time, the restaurants and hotels were lackadaisical. In 1918, the law was enforced by prosecutions; if found guilty, businesses would be forced to close for one day.

On the other side of Biscayne Bay stood a barrier island filled with swamp rats, thick mangroves and even more dreams. The land was the island of Miami Beach. At first, grand dreams of coconut and avocado plantations were set for the land, but after failed attempts, the settlers of the island set to make it a paradise resort and real-estate haven. The longest wooden bridge in the country was commissioned by John Collins and provided easier access to the island. It opened in 1913, and in 1915, John Collins, the Lummus brothers and Carl Fisher incorporated the city of Miami Beach with three hundred residents. The beach's first common hotel, Brown's, was located on Ocean Drive and First Street. Today, it is the home of the celebrity favorite Prime One Twelve. The hotel is also still in operation, though it offers only nine rooms.

Hotel Royal Palm breakfast menu on Wednesday, February 27, 1901. *Courtesy of the New York Public Library System, Miss Frank E. Buttolph American Menu Collection, 1851–1930.*

HOTEL ROYAL PALM

MIAMI BISCAYNE BAY
FLORIDA

Luncheon

1 to 2.30

Puree a la Soubise   Cold Consomme in Cups

Young Green Onions   Radishes   Queen Olives
Sliced Tomatoes   Heinz's Gherkins

Whiting, Nut Brown Butter

Boiled Fresh Beef, Horseradish Sauce
Calf's Head en Tortue
Lobster, en caisse, a la Newburg

Boiled New and Mashed Potatoes
Stewed Tomatoes   Turnips in Cream   String Beans
Corn Fritters   Spinach a la Creme

COLD
Roast Beef   Ham   Tongue   Young Turkey
Lamb   Pickled Pig's Feet   Corned Beef
  Tongue   Chipped Beef

Chicken Salad

Farina Pudding, Rhine Wine Sauce
Apple Pie   Boston Cream Puffs   Assorted Cakes
Vanilla Ice Cream

Red Currant Jelly   Sliced Fresh Pineapple

Cheese   Crackers
Tea   Fresh Milk   Coffee

The Swimming Pool is open daily, except Sunday.

Sunday, January 27, 1901   Henry W. Merrill, Manager

Hotel Royal Palm luncheon menu on Thursday, January 27, 1901.
Courtesy of the New York Public Library System, Miss Frank E. Buttolph American Menu Collection, 1851–1930.

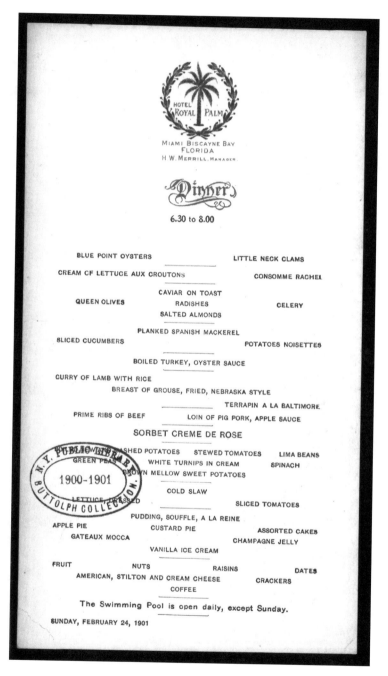

Hotel Royal Palm dinner menu on Sunday, February 24, 1901. *Courtesy of the New York Public Library System, Miss Frank E. Buttolph American Menu Collection, 1851–1930.*

One of Miami Beach's earliest food pioneers was Joseph "Joe" Weiss of the famed Joe's Stone Crab. Joe came to South Florida in 1913 for health reasons, and Miami Beach did the trick for him. He brought over his wife and son and began with a lunch stand at Smith's bathing casino. In 1918, the family purchased a bungalow in the same neighborhood and began serving food on the front porch—they called it Joe's Restaurant. They didn't serve the famous stone crabs until 1921 but began by serving snapper, pompano, crawfish, mackerel and some meat dishes. The restaurant's website notes, "When we started serving them [stone crabs] cracked with hash brown potatoes, coleslaw and mayonnaise, they were an instant success. We charged seventy-five cents for four or five crabs, twenty-five cents for potatoes and twenty-five cents an order for coleslaw. And this is the way we have been serving them since." Joe's celebrated its 100th anniversary in 2012 and continues to be a shining example of the immigrant success story. No trip to Miami is complete without a trip to the iconic restaurant. A favorite among the A-list celebrities, Joe's is open only for the stone crab season, which runs from October to May. In the off months, the to-go section is available and offers other delicious items from the menu, including their famous key lime pie.

MIAMI'S OLDEST BAR: TOBACCO ROAD

Operating under a number of aliases and operations (some illegal), this 101-year-old bar has had a rich and interesting history. Opened in 1912, Tobacco Road was a bakery that fronted as a speakeasy. A secret room on the second floor housed the liquor. Located on the river, it was the perfect location for serving contraband and was extremely popular during Miami's dry periods and Prohibition. The bar changed hands several times and did not operate under the name Tobacco Road until the 1940s. Throughout the years, it carried such names as Chicken Roost, Chanticleer Restaurant and Sandiclere. In the 1940s, it was owned by a New Yorker and nationally known as a scandalous gay bar. Miami, then a prudish city, eventually shut it down. The present owners have owned it since 1982. Due to its location in the heart of Brickell, the 1980s were not great for Tobacco Road. Miami residents were scared of going to downtown Miami, and the bar was truly a dive bar, catering to a rough crowd. But the bar reclaimed its jazzy revival in the late 1990s and early 2000s and now thrives as a landmark for patrons of all kinds, from the happy-hour downtown business crowd to the hippie Coconut Grove residents. It is also a champion for localism, reviving and promoting Miami's local music and food-truck scenes. It also serves pub fare and is known for its sandwiches and other cheap but tasty fare.

Chapter 4

1920s-1940s

THE 1920s

Miami experienced a great boom in both tourism and population in the early 1920s. The *Miami Herald* was one of the heaviest newspapers in the country as a result of its extensive land advertisement section aimed at attracting settlers to the area. A mastermind PR man and one of Miami's founding pioneers, Everest G. Sewell even commissioned a large billboard on Forty-second Street in Times Square to attract hoards of people to the area. But as with any boom, a bust always follows. The boom reached its peak in 1925, but the crash came just a year later after the Hurricane of 1926, propelling Miami into the Great Depression four years earlier than the rest of the country. The discovery of the Mediterranean fruit fly in 1929 killed the citrus industry and cut production rates in half. This did not help the situation.

Why did Miami intrigue so many people? Aside from being the premier resort on the East Coast, the area was also sold as a healthful place. The 1920s were a prosperous time around the country, and people had more disposable income. At the very beginning, Miami offered much hope for get-rich-quick schemes.

The boom led to the creation of many communities, including Coral Gables, Miami Shores, Hialeah, Miami Springs and Opa-Locka. The city limits of Miami also grew in size with the annexation of various communities including Coconut Grove, Silver Bluff and Lemon City.

The first Chinese-American restaurant in the area opened inside of the McKinnon Hotel in 1920 and was named Wo Kee & Son Co. With a seating capacity for two hundred people, the restaurant served both Chinese and American dishes. The dishes were prepared by a Chinese chef and also featured afternoon tea, and because the restaurant was located inside of the hotel, it was open for breakfast, lunch and dinner. The 1920s was a boom decade with an overwhelming influx of new people, mainly from the North. In the beginning, there was a large influx of ethnic populations of Syrians, Lebanese, Greeks, Italians and Jews—all bringing with them the foods of their culture. Notable restaurants of this decade include the Leon de Leon on Ocean Drive and Second Street, with the best spaghetti in town; Gallat Court's Café; and the Brickell. The Brickell was the hit sensation of the 1921 season, and top socialites from around the country came specifically for the grand opening. The menu on that night included fresh shrimp cocktail, chicken a la printaniere, broiled Spanish mackerel, julienne potatoes, filet mignon with mushrooms, French-fried potatoes, roast young chicken with cranberry sauce, potatoes au gratin, French peas, Waldorf salad, English plum pudding, hot mince pie, French pastries, cigars and cigarettes. Over the next nine years, mansions were erected in Miami Beach, and Collins Avenue was considered Millionaire's Row. At the end of the decade, the city even got its very own Coca-Cola bottling plant in present-day Wynwood on NW Twenty-ninth Street and Third Avenue, setting the lay of the land for what was to become the Miami industrial and warehouse hub.

Another notable hotel of the decade was the Biltmore. The Biltmore Hotel opened to the public on January 14, 1926. Drinks were available at the grand opening even though Prohibition was in full effect. From it's opening, it instantly gained international appeal. A London columnist named Nat Gubbins visited the hotel in his travels and introduced a pre-luncheon drink at the Cascades Bar: half port, half brandy, with a twist and no ice, served in a wine glass. The drink was appropriately named after him and could be ordered as an off-the-menu item for many years after. Unfortunately, it eventually died off, as it is no longer known by the bar staff. During the years of war, the hotel was used as an infirmary and training facility for soldiers. On January 16, 1987, a historical dinner was held to commemorate the preservation of the hotel. During the Biltmore Hotel Preservation Ball, diners feasted on the original opening-night menu, which consisted of coupe andalouse followed by turtle soup, poached halibut parsley, Noilly Prat sauce, medallion of veal with foie gras, truffle Armagnac sauce and salad, ending with fresh Strawberries Romanoff. Famous visitors to the Biltmore include Al Capone, Judy Garland and the Vanderbilts.

Burdine's

Burdine's, also known as the Florida Store, was purchased by Macy's in 2004, although many who grew up in Miami still refer to it as Burdine's. Although a department store, Burdine's also had a long food history. From the rooftop garden to the Men's Grill, Tea Room and lunch counter, Burdine's was popular with downtown Miami's eating crowd. A popular item among girls at the Tea Room was called the Snow Princess ice cream, which consisted of "a whipped cream skirt over a cone of ice cream with a ceramic princess doll top." Geraldine Williams recalled:

> *The rare privilege of being out of school* [Riverside or Ada Merritt] *and going with my dressed-up mother to lunch at one of these tearooms, where models meandered in and through the tables showing the latest clothes, made me feel very grown up. The waitresses all had fancy cotton handkerchiefs pinned to their uniform bodice in corsage fashion behind their nametag and, as I remember, were very serious and gracious. No one called my mother "honey" or was too busy to bring an extra patty of ice-cold butter on a lace doily. It was all very genteel.*[19]

THE 1930S

After the drama of the end of the boom in 1926 and the subsequent Hurricane of 1926, Miami was ready to be in the sunshine again. Having experienced its own version of the Great Depression in 1926, Miami did not feel the full impact of the true Great Depression as badly as the rest of the country and came out of the era much earlier than its counterparts in 1935. But that is not to say that the city wasn't affected. During this period, Miami had only one surviving bank in operation, First National Bank, but the positives and optimism outweighed the negatives. Aiding in the boost of the area was the sudden emergence of the air transportation industry, and Miami became the hub for National Airlines, Eastern Airlines and Pan Am Airlines, further increasing the boom in tourism. Additionally, people from the North wanted to escape their dreary lives. Miami Beach experienced another building boom, and the world was introduced to the style of Art Deco in the forms of hotels such as the Winter Haven, Congress and the Hotel Victor.

One of the beach's first inhabitants, Malvina Weiss Liebman Gutschmidt, recalled her experiences on the beach:

The Beach was like a South Sea Island then. We ate all our meals right on the beach…practically lived on the beach. We'd pile up driftwood and ferns and burn them at the full moon. We swam in the phosphorescence and fished all day—my brothers wove their own cast nets. Maybe you took a fishing trip to the Seven Seas for a dollar a day or played canasta or bridge on the hotel porch or got dressed up in white gloves and a hat to visit Lincoln Road, the Rue de la Paix of the South, making a long window shopping tour from Washington Avenue to Alton Road, then back again. If you were staying at an efficiency apartment for the season, Washington Avenue was the place to shop for dinner, lined with fish stores, kosher butchers, delicatessens, bakeries, greengrocers, the Piggly Wiggly. Few of the hotels had dining rooms, so if you were staying in a hotel, you probably ate out on Washington Avenue, too, where you could find some of the greatest names in New York and Atlantic City cafeteria and kosher cuisine. Maybe you'd see Al Jolson eating "flannel cakes" (waffles) at Bob Feinstein's, Manny's or some other celebrity at Winnie's Waffle Shop on Twenty-third and Collins, which stayed open till three or four in the morning for a post-gambling nosh. Holleman's, Hoffman's, the Southern, and the Waldorf cafeterias all did a brisk business catering to thrifty South Beach tourists. Teddy's on Ocean Drive, between Tenth and Eleventh, advertised seven courses for 65 cents "under the tropical sky with the surf at your feet." Without the surf, you could get the same for 50 cents at the Roxy on 12 Street. Wheelan's Fish Grill ("Out of the Ocean, Into the Pan") offered fish, salad, roll, and coffee for $1. In the oldest area of the beach, south of Fifth Street, open-front stores sold souvenirs; shell knickknacks; pecan baskets; assortments of tangerine marmalades and coconut patties; masks made from carved, painted coconut husks; and souvenir neckties.[20]

Nationally, one-pot meals such as macaroni and cheese and chili became popular due to the scarcity of food. There was also a growth in the

Various restaurant advertisements in *Miami News*.

consumption of "bad" foods like hot dogs and hamburgers, and meatloaf was the go-to meat choice for cooking mothers. Locally, the food trends of the decade revolved around fresh fish houses, delis, southern food and good ol' American diners and restaurants serving hearty food at affordable prices. During times of hardship, a return to the land is in order, and Miami had an advantage in this category, as its roots were in farming and agriculture—another reason why Miami boomed in the second half of the 1930s. At this time, Miami was a southern city that placed great emphasis on southern cuisine and regional Florida cooking. As Miami moved away from a farming and fishing community toward a vibrant city, many new people came to the city with their own traditions and customs. The following decades saw a significant change in the local restaurant world, with an increase in dining out and updated menus to cater to the changing demographics. Popular

A Regal Beer newspaper advertisement from the August 22, 1947 issue of *Miami News*.

restaurants of the decade included the Howard Johnson Restaurant and BM Diner, both on Biscayne Boulevard; Captain Tom's Restaurant on the Miami River; and Hoffman's Cafeteria on Espanola Way and Collins. Infamous openings included East Coast Fisheries Restaurant & Market, Wagner Brewing Company, S&S Diner (opened by Greek immigrants) and The Forge, of which the last two are still in existence and are two of the longest standing restaurants in Miami.

Open through 2000, East Coast Fisheries was the largest rival to Joe's Stone Crab, offering the very best in seafood. One of its most famous advertisements

Roney Plaza chef Joseph Amblard putting raw crawfish in the Radarange, Miami Beach, Florida. *Courtesy of the State Archives of Florida, Florida Memory Project.*

was: "If it swims, we have it." Wagner Brewing Company was Miami's first brewery. It was eventually purchased by American Brewing Company out of New Orleans in 1939 and began brewing Regal Beer, a lager. (If you spell regal backwards, you get the word "lager.") "Perfect for hot Miami" was one of the beer's unofficial slogans. Regal Beer was discontinued, and Wagner Brewing Company eventually went out of business, but Miamians continued their loving relationship with beer. Wynwood Brewing Company, set to open in 2013, hopes to bring back the spirit of hometown craft brewery to the city. The Forge opened in the former spot of a blacksmith shop. From its inception, the restaurant's specialty was steak. Alvin Malnik purchased the restaurant in 1968, remodeled it completely and reopened it in 1969. His son Shareef took over in 1991 and again closed the restaurant for the infamous remodel and menu overhaul of 2009, reopening with Chef Dewey LoSasso, who spent an estimated twelve weeks researching the original menu. Also popular during this time was people watching from the sidewalk café at Café de la Paix at the Roney Plaza, which originally opened in 1926. Ann Armbruster wrote of the scene, "…women in light sundresses or white sharkskin trousers, turbans and sunglasses, the men in tropical-weight suits came to lunch beneath the big polka-dot umbrellaed tables."[21] And if you ever want a trip back in time, the S&S Diner has not changed a bit.

THE PROHIBITION ERA IN MIAMI

Even before Prohibition began nationally, Miami had its battles with alcohol consumption. The city seesawed between dry and wet from the city's birth in 1896 up until the official start of Prohibition, with varying degrees of police enforcement and non-enforcement. As for its residents, Miami was always meant to be a wet city, and their blatant disregard for the law at all times is the perfect example of this.

As part of the contract between Henry Flagler and Julia Tuttle, anti-liquor clauses were added onto all land deeds, preventing landowners from buying, selling or manufacturing liquor. The penalty for violating this clause? The land would be promptly taken away.

Still, the anti-liquor clauses did not stop residents from scoring the hooch or searching for the booze. It is said that the bootlegging business boomed during the time between 1896 and 1919, only further increasing during the Prohibition era and therefore making Miami the most important city in the United States. Soon after the city's incorporation, saloons opened up steps from the city limits in North Miami. North Miami was a shantytown, a hub for saloons, prostitution and gambling.

The temperance movements of the 1880s, including the Anti-Saloon League and Woman's Christian Temperance Union (most commonly referred to as the WCTU), started the wave that would eventually lead to the formalization of Prohibition. It was fairly popular at the turn of the century for local alcohol prohibition laws to be placed in effect. For example, in 1916, twenty-three out of forty-eight states had adopted anti-saloon legislations and were even able to eradicate near-beer saloons, establishments that sold beer containing less than 2 percent alcohol. In Miami, a law like this was passed in 1913.

Carrie Nation, one of the country's most fervent and outspoken characters in the temperance movement, even made an appearance during those trying times in Miami. A March 13, 1908 article in the *Miami News* reported that there were two thousand supporters in attendance for her speech. An extremely religious woman, Nation noted that the Bible condemned alcohol and that in her findings of the city, Miami was an extremely corrupt place. She is best known for her rampant scenes at liquor-yielding establishments, including saloons, where she would smash whole kegs and use stones and bricks to break bottles. Her most popular story about Miami is when she went undercover to purchase alcohol at saloons on Sunday (the law prohibited liquor sales on Sundays) and was able to purchase it freely in North Miami. While Miami had a past of disregarding the law, her visit did do some good. The months following her visit led to stricter liquor laws and increased police enforcement. This would eventually die out after the start of formal Prohibition.

Before 1913, Broward and Miami were part of the same county. In an anti-liquor vote of 1913, votes for a dry county prevailed because more residents from the north voted—the north in this case being Broward County. Broward as a whole was a dry county, while Miami was considered a wet county. The dry clause passed, but not without a fight, and these repeals are what eventually led to the distinct separation of Broward County from Miami-Dade County. The Prohibition law passed in 1919 but did not take effect until 1920. The first section of the amendment read:

> *After one year from the ratification of this article, the manufacture, sale, or transportation of intoxicating liquors within, the importation thereof into, or the exportation thereof from the United States and all territory subject to the jurisdiction thereof for beverage purposes is hereby prohibited.*

It is important to note the exact terms of this new law. It was illegal to manufacture or distribute alcoholic beverages, but it was not illegal to possess it for personal use. You could still use it at home as long as it stayed inside and it was not gifted, traded or sold.

Naturally, this era is infamous for the rise of speakeasies, home distillers, bootleggers and rumrunners, gambling and prostitution. There was also a rise in the number of women that drank and organized crime, most popularly seen in Miami because of Al Capone's residence on the Miami Beach islands. During his residence in Miami, Capone was constantly in and out of jail. Again, for alcohol-related purposes, Miami was the most important city during this time. With its close proximity to the water and the Caribbean Islands, Miami was the gateway for rumrunning in the country. It also boasted vast open swamps, inlets, and mangroves, making it easy to hide and escape. In a tug of war, local law enforcers turned a blind eye, while national organizations enforced stricter laws, setting up anti-rumrunning headquarters in the city and its surrounding waters. But this was all contradictory, as President Warren G. Harding shared several drinks with Carl Fisher after his inauguration in 1921 during his visit to Miami Beach. "Costing only four dollars at the original point of sale, at the height of Prohibition a case of Cuban rum sold for one hundred dollars or more once it hit Florida beaches."[22] What did they smuggle? Caribbean rum, English gin and Scotch whiskey were the most popular. Once rumrummers crossed the "rum line," an actual line located three miles off the coast, American law no longer had any power. The Bahamas, Bimini, Cuba and Jamaica all played key roles in the rumrunning of booze.

One of the more interesting stories out of the Prohibition era came from a man named Thomas J. Peters. Sally ling wrote of Peters:

> *The Miami City Directory estimated that 150,000 tourists would visit the "Magic City" during 1919. To satisfy their thirst, Thomas J. Peters, a wealthy tomato farmer and owner of Miami's Halcyon Hotel, convened a group of friends from the Miami Angler's Club to develop an exclusive hotel—the Bimini Bay Rod and Gun Club—on the island of Bimini in the Bahamas. Designed as an alternative to the illegal activities of running booze from the Bahamas into South Florida, Peter's plan called for bringing thirsty consumers to a posh Bimini resort where drinking was legal.*[23]

Unfortunately, Peters's plan never came to fruition, and it quickly became clear that rumrunning was the only option.

Another infamous story involves the great concrete ship *Sapona*. The product was kept on schooners anchored between Bimini and Cat Cay, the most infamous being the SS *Sapona*, owned by rum baron Bruce Bethel. In a great storm of the 1920s, the ship and its cargo—millions of dollars worth of booze—was destroyed. This forced bootleggers to permanently move their operations to Bimini, whose economy and crime rate experienced a

Police destroying confiscated liquor. *Courtesy of the State Archives of Florida, Florida Memory Project.*

notable boom. It was a never-ending party on the island. Prohibition was repealed in 1933.

CHARLES BAKER JR.

One of the most interesting early residents of Coconut Grove was Charles H. Baker Jr. Both an extensive writer and traveler in his time, Baker can be compared to an early version of Anthony Bourdain. His most famous book, *The Gentleman's Companion: Being An Exotic Cookery Book*, was published in 1939, and the dedication on the book's first pages was the first of its kind. The dedication? To the stomach. Food-wise, Baker was enlightened. He surrounded himself with equally interesting people, including sportsmen, explorers, musicians, scientists, vagabonds and writers—all of whom were interested in good things to eat and drink and cared for the exotic and intriguing ways of composing said eats and drinks. In his book, food is described as the guiding light during the Depression and early times of the war.

It's interesting to note that even though a plethora of popular cookbooks existed and were marketed toward women at this time, they were considered bad cooks. Additionally, the trend in more complicated cookery was growing during this era, as was imagination and the need for adventure. While routine cookery books were the most common, professional books were available but were generally more detailed and complicated.

On page nineteen of *The Gentleman's Companion*, Baker describes the process of the proper form of preparing a suckling pig:

> *Suckling pig done in the true Polish style, and contrary to usual American customer, served cold and boiled—not roasted and hot. This dish was recommended to us by a random and unruly associate who distinguished himself by disembarking both himself and a motor car of parts at the northernmost tip of Norway and driving the blooming thing all over the Scandinavias, Finland, Poland and into Russia, where, with other more important things, it was impounded by some of Mr. Stalin's right bowers. His final instruction was to chill the meat very cold before serving. Instead of cooking whole, have the animal jointed. Cover with cold water—no herbs or seasonings or whatever, just water! Salt is added 10 minutes before taking off the fire—just why, neither our friend nor his Polish informants could satisfactorily explain. This should be after from 1½ to 2 hours, depending on size of piglet. Chill cold as possible, serve sliced with chilled horseradish sauce made by grating fresh horseradish (under no condition employ the stale bottled type!) and mixing in the following proportion: ¼ cup horseradish, 1 tbsp tarragon vinegar and 1 cup sour cream. Cold tart white wine is in order, rather than the more conventional red.[24]*

THE 1940S

While the rest of the country was being catapulted from the Great Depression straight into World War II, Miami was still booming from the second part of the 1930s. And while other parts of Florida were negatively affected by the war, Miami was not hurt too much. Just as it did during World War I, the United States government used Miami as a training base camp for the troops. This influx of troops brought further blips of boom as the city's population grew and spending increased. Miami was a popular location for training due to its warm weather and the fact that its low-lying ground lent to easy year-round training. While the era was prosperous, Miami still had to abide by the rationing laws of the country, which led to a temporary return to area's farming and agricultural roots. As previously mentioned in other sections of this book, this was relatively simple for Miami, which had never strayed far from its agricultural roots.

Nationally, the U.S. government restricted meat, sugar, butter, cheese, eggs and coffee. Margarine was invented as a replacement for butter. Women also began to have a bigger place in the workforce, which meant less time for cooking meals at home. The invention of Tupperware eased this transition, and military research led to the public introduction of instant coffee. Locally, European bakeries, Jewish delis and small restaurants with family-style meals were popular. And while going to restaurants was more popular than before, people still did not eat out regularly. It was considered a treat to go out, and diners would save it for a special occasion, donning their finest wear during these trips.

Popular restaurants of the decade included Smitty's Restaurant, Coopertown Restaurant, Fox's Sherron Inn, Paramount Soda Shop and Zink's Luncheonette. Popular hotels of the decade included the Delano, National Hotel, Saxony, Sans Souci and Pan American Hotel. The Delano and the National hotels are still in operation today and are as popular as ever. The end of the Great Depression boosted the development of hotels—out went the promoters, and in came the more seasoned hotel men that created prosperous, beautiful hotels that functioned properly and lasted for years.

Coopertown Restaurant is still in existence out in the Everglades, serving traditional Florida fare such as frog legs, catfish and gator tail. Gatti's Restaurant was also extremely popular during this decade. Opened in 1925 on 1427 West Avenue, Gatti's was an institution on the beach. In 1992, the restaurant closed after sixty-seven years in service. In the '90s, Gatti's was no longer considered hip or trendy, and the old-school restaurant lost its charm and its place in the hustle and bustle of the celebrity-driven world. The Delano opened in the later part of the decade and still stands as an icon on the beach. Most recently (and to the detriment of many), Bianca replaced

Vintage postcard of Shangri-La, a popular restaurant in the 1940s. *Courtesy of CardCow.com.*

the famous Blue Door restaurant, bringing back the stuffy and snobby dining frequently seen in the '90s.

Another popular icon of the decade that spilled out into the 1950s was Georgette's Tea Room, housed in a thirteen-room building that also served as a hotel. Georgette's was the place for the affluent black community to meet. Billie Holiday was known to frequent the spot, along with Nat King Cole and Bessie Smith. Located in Brownsville and owned by Georgette Scott Campbell, the hotel offered accommodations to many of the black entertainers who frequently came to perform at many of the beach's hotels. Segregation did not allow for them to stay in hotels on the beach, and the city of Overtown provided a refuge for them. The Mary Elizabeth Hotel, also in Overtown, also offered accommodations to prominent performers of the time. Count Basie and Jackie Robinson were noted to have stayed at the hotel. One of the fancier hotels in the area, it was closed down after desegregation, and the historic landmark was eventually demolished, destroying a historic marker in Miami's timeline.

There is no better way to understand the eating habits of a decade or a generation than by studying cookbooks. Here you will find the most amusing, albeit helpful, anecdotes and tips ranging in topics from the mundane to dieting, party planning and beyond. Following are some helpful tips for around the household from *The Miami Woman's Club Cook Book* (1944):

> *A few drops of vinegar added to the boiling water in which an egg is to be poached will prevent the egg from breaking.*
>
> *Tomato catsup poured over roasting pork gives the pork a fine flavor.*
>
> *Squeeze a little lemon juice in your rice to help bleach it and give it a better flavor.*
>
> *If you place a little sugar in the teapot before you make tea, the tablecloth will not stain if you should spill any of the tea.*
>
> *When cooking cauliflower, if a piece of stale bread or a well-toasted crust is placed on top of it, all disagreeable odors will be eliminated.*

Concern for the figure has been around as long as the excesses of eating have been around. In the same 1944 cookbook, there is an example of a strict diet for those that want to lose a couple of pounds. The diet lacks variety and combination of flavors and today would be a difficult one to follow. Weight is easily lost because the calorie intake is extremely low. If you are to try this now, proceed with caution.

EIGHTEEN-DAY REDUCING DIET

All material in this section was submitted by Dr. James D. Orr, P.T., Dietitian and Physio-Therapist of the Gateway Health Institute, Kansas City, Missouri. Before using any diet, we recommend that you consult a physician.

Breakfast: In this diet, the same breakfast is used every day and consists of: ½ grapefruit, Melba toast, coffee

Note: Melba toast is dry bread toasted without butter.

1ˢᵗ Day
Lunch: ½ grapefruit, 1 egg, 6 slices cucumber, 1 slice Melba toast, tea or coffee
Dinner: 2 eggs, 1 tomato, ½ head lettuce, ½ grapefruit, coffee

2ⁿᵈ Day
Lunch: 1 orange, 1 egg, 1 slice Melba toast, ½ head lettuce, tea
Dinner: 1 small broiled steak, ½ head lettuce, 1 tomato, ½ grapefruit, tea or coffee

3ʳᵈ Day
Lunch: ½ grapefruit, 1 egg, 8 slices cucumber, tea or coffee
Dinner: 1 lamp chop lean, plain, 1 egg, 3 radishes, ½ grapefruit, tea or coffee

4ᵗʰ Day
Lunch: 1 tomato, ½ grapefruit, 1 slice Melba toast, cottage cheese, tea
Dinner: ½ grapefruit, water cress, 1 small broiled steak, coffee

5ᵗʰ Day
Lunch: 1 orange, 1 lamb chop, ½ head lettuce, tea
Dinner: ½ grapefruit, 1 tomato, 2 eggs, ½ head lettuce, tea

6th Day
Lunch: 1 egg, 1 orange, tea
Dinner: 1 poached egg, 1 slice Melba toast, 1 orange, tea

7th Day
Lunch: ½ grapefruit, 1 egg, ½ head lettuce, 1 tomato, 2 olives
Dinner: 1 lamb chop plain, 6 slices cucumber, 2 olives, 1 tomato, tea or coffee

8th Day
Lunch: 1 broiled lamb chop, ½ head lettuce, ½ grapefruit, coffee
Dinner: 1 egg, 1 serving spinach, plain, ½ grapefruit, 1 slice Melba toast, tea

9th Day
Lunch: 1 egg, 1 tomato, ½ grapefruit, tea
Dinner: any meat salad

10th Day
Lunch: ½ grapefruit, 1 lamb chop plain, ½ head lettuce, tea
Dinner: ½ grapefruit, 1 lamb chop plain, ½ head lettuce, tea

11th Day
Lunch: 1 slice cinnamon toast, tea
Dinner: 1 small broiled steak, 1 stalk celery, 1 tomato, 2 olives, tea

12th Day
Lunch: ½ lobster, 2 crackers, ½ grapefruit, tea
Dinner: 1 broiled steak, plain coleslaw, 1 tomato, 1 orange

13th Day
Lunch: 1 egg, 1 slice Melba toast, ½ grapefruit
Dinner: ½ grapefruit, 1 small broiled steak, ½ head lettuce, 1 stalk celery, coffee

14th Day
Lunch: 1 egg, 1 tomato, ½ grapefruit, 1 slice Melba toast
Dinner: 1 lamb chop, ½ tablespoonful catsup, 1 slice Melba toast, ½ grapefruit

15th Day
Lunch: 1 egg, 1 slice Melba toast, ½ grapefruit, coffee
Dinner: 1 small broiled steak, 1 small portion spinach, 1 orange, tea

16th Day
Lunch: 1 egg, 1 tomato, ½ grapefruit, coffee
Dinner: 1 small white fish (broiled), 1 small portion spinach, plain, 1 orange, tea

17th Day
Lunch: 1 lamb chop, ½ head lettuce, ½ grapefruit, tea
Dinner: 1 small broiled steak, 1 tomato, 1 stalk celery, coffee

18th Day:
Lunch: 1 chicken leg (broiled), 1 tomato, ½ grapefruit, 1 glass lemonade (no sugar)
Dinner: ½ can pink salmon, 1 serving spinach, ½ grapefruit, coffee

Note: You may substitute fish or the white meat of chicken any time for the lamb. If you have not lost the desired weight, you will repeat until you have lost the weight you wish. This diet takes the weight off slowly, but you do not become flabby. Oranges may be substituted for grapefruit.

Cookbooks are also great as a teaching tool. 1944's *Florida Seafood Cookery*, published by the Florida Department of Agriculture, offers a myriad of useful information regarding fish, including how to purchase it, cook it, butcher it and classify it. The following list divides fish into "lean" and "fat" categories and denotes the best time of year to catch them:

LEAN AND FAT FLORIDA FISHES

LEAN
Bluefish: Year round
Blue pike: March–December
Carp: April–December
Crappie: Year-round
Croker (hardhead): Year-round
Drum: November–June
Flounder: November–May
Grouper: November–May
Kingfish: January–June
King whiting: Year-round
Mullet (popeye): Year-round
Sea bass (black fish): Year-round
Sheepshead: Year-round
Sunfish: December–June
Swordfish: June–October
Weakfish (sea trout): April–November
White bass: Year-round
Whiting (silver hake): May–December
Yellow perch: Year-round

FAT
Barracuda: February–June
Catfish: Year-round
Eel: Year-round
Mackerel (Spanish): November–May
Pompano: Year-round
Porgie: Year-round
Scup: Year-round
Shad: Year-round
Whitefish: April–December

Additional recipes include cucumber sauce, caper sauce, brown sauce, scalloped oysters, broiled crawfish, crab gumbo, sautéed king mackerel, fish pie, creamed shrimp, fried mullet southern style.

Another such book brought out to the public but geared specifically toward the commercial kitchen in promoting and guiding chefs and restaurateurs to use fruits and vegetables in their menus was 1931's *Florida Fruits and Vegetables in the Commercial Menu*, also published by the Florida Department of Agriculture. Examples of topics from the table of contents include the effect of heat on green vegetables, Florida "greens" varieties and preparation, fruits identification and uses, fruit zones in Florida, fresh fruits in the menu, place in the menu, fruit jellies or molds and frozen fruits, Florida salads in the menu, a vitamin table, citrus and health, what to do with leftovers, sample vegetable plates/platters, methods of preparation and meal pairings. The cookbook not only provides recipes for chefs but also discusses different flavor profiles and the reasoning as to why certain fruits pair well with savory items, as well as plating and garnishing suggestions. Below are two examples:

FLORIDA DESSERT SALAD
Setting: Lettuce leaves with watercress
Center: Hole preserved figs, drained and stuffed with cream or cottage cheese
Garnish: Pecans
Note: Fresh Florida sugar figs should be used when in season

FLORIDA FRUIT SPECIAL
Setting: Escarole, Florida's loose lettuce
Fruit: Pink grapefruit with strawberries
Dressing: French with fruit juice or French cream dressing

Chapter 5

1950s-1970s

THE 1950S

By the 1950s, Florida's ethnic pressure center had shifted to Miami. Since the 1920s, large numbers of Cubans had been coming to Miami for vacations, while nervous Cuban officials and businessmen invested heavily in South Florida real estate.[25]

At the end of World War II, there was a spirited revival in the United States. This was good for the evolution and prosperity of the country, but food-wise, this revival came with negative implications. The development of highways brought about the rise of fast-food joints and increased production of processed foods. This decade also saw the upshot of ethnic cuisines throughout the country due to the soldiers, having been abroad, wanting to continue eating the foods they thoroughly enjoyed in Europe and Asia. Popular dishes of the decade included beef stroganoff, steak Diane, beef wellington, iceberg wedge salad, fondue, Bundt cake and casseroles. The 1950s also saw the introduction of products such as Tang and dehydrated Lipton onion soup mix.

Locally, Miami experienced the same international and ethnic interest. There was an increase in both the interest in and opening of many Italian and Asian restaurants. Popular restaurants of the decade included Embers, Edith & Fritz, The Great Gables Drive-In, Shorty's BBQ, Allen's Drug Store and Mei Yin Chinese Restaurant. Miami also got its first White Castle in 1959.

Everyone loved Embers Restaurant. In the 1950s, Embers was the place to go if you wanted a good steak, and people came from all over for a taste of its secret orange-colored French dressing. Located on Twenty-second Street and Collins Avenue, the restaurant ironically burned down in 1984. So dearly missed, a copycat was erected on the same spot in the 1990s, serving the same food, including apple fritters, stuffed baked potatoes, duck, a chicken-and-rib combo, white bean soup, potato-leek soup and creamed spinach alongside modern additions such as tuna medallions, salmon with mustard dill dip, baked red snapper with lime and veal chops. The owners, also old customers of the original 1950s restaurant, tried to perfectly emulate the same ambiance. Sadly, the idea did not transcend. The Miami food scene of the '90s was on a different plane.

EMBER'S FAMOUS FRENCH DRESSING

Ingredients:
2 cups mayonnaise
½ cup ketchup
½ cup sour cream
¼ cup sweet pickle juice (from a jar of sweet pickles)
¼ cup orange juice
2 garlic cloves, crushed
1 teaspoon yellow mustard
½ cup sugar
1 teaspoon paprika
Juice of 2 lemons
1 tablespoon Worcestershire sauce
1 hard-cooked egg (optional)
A few black olives (optional)

Preparation:
Process the mayonnaise, ketchup, sour cream, pickle juice, orange juice, garlic, mustard, sugar, paprika, lemon juice and Worcestershire sauce in a blender for just a second or two. Refrigerate 24 hours before serving. If you like, chop the egg fine and garnish salad plates with egg and olives. Makes about 2 ¾ cups dressing.

"In 1959, Miami was glitzy, gauche, and a city on the edge of crisis. Miami was home to large numbers of aging Jews and young blacks. African American leaders expressed anger at Miami's insensitivities toward poverty, education, and a Jim Crow color line. Precisely at the moment the civil rights revolution unfolded, Miami experience its own upheaval."[26] The last day of the end of this decade set off a chain of events that forever changed Miami—implications that can still be seen in the present day. The Cuban Revolution was one of the most important moments in the history of Miami—just as important as the extension of Flagler's railroad. Fidel Castro's conquest of Cuba on January 1, 1960, opened the floodgates for half a million Cubans to come to Miami. Up until this point, American Southern, Jewish, Italian and spurts of German and Asian influences could sum up the mainstay cuisines of the city. What followed was exciting but forever changed the demographics of the city, as mass influxes of newcomers forced out settlers in the area and caused displacement elsewhere.

Two of the decade's most important restaurants were Jumbo's Restaurant and Jamaica Inn. Jumbo's opened in 1955 and was located on what is considered the Seventh Avenue Corridor, which included such favorites as Carino's Italian, Latta's, Toby's Cafeteria and Gracie's Italian. The restaurant was a hotbed for the civil rights movement and in 1966 was the first restaurant in the city to integrate.

Off the mainland, on Key Biscayne, a piece of Jamaica was deemed a must when traveling to Florida, and the Jamaica Inn was honored as one of America's Outstanding Restaurants by the *Ford Times*. According to a September 1953 article in the *Miami Daily News*, the restaurant was built by Hugh Matheson so that he didn't have to trek to the West Indies for roast beef and Yorkshire pudding. The Inn proved to be a true slice of Jamaica in our gem of a city. The copy on restaurant advertising pieces gives a great description of one of the more interesting items of fauna in the center of the restaurant:

> *Here you may dine while overlooking a patio flourishing with equatorial plants—the same plants so familiar to the island of Jamaica from which the Inn derives its name. Most intriguing of all the patio plants is the breadfruit tree, distinguished by its large, graceful leaf. Introduced into the Caribbean during the 16th century as a staple diet for slaves, the breadfruit is almost a stranger to the U.S. In fact, Jamaica Inn's breadfruit tree is one of two known to be flourishing north of Key West, Florida.*

The restaurant once located on 320 Crandon Boulevard is now a park.

Above: The Fontainebleau's restaurant advertisements in *Miami News.*

Opposite, top: A vintage brochure showing the Fontainebleau's various restaurants. *Courtesy of Fontainebleau Miami Beach.*

Opposite, bottom: Dining room scene at the Fontainebleau. *Courtesy of Fontainebleau Miami Beach.*

Popular hotels of the decade included the DiLido, Algiers, Empress, Casablanca, Overtown's Lord Calvert Hotel, Booker Terrace Motel, Fontainebleau and the Eden Roc. One of the best hotel wars of the decade came with the building of two eponymous hotels, the Fontainebleau and the Eden Roc. What's interesting is that although Morris Lapidus designed both

Chez Bon Bon

This is the Coffee Shop *élégant* . . .
where delicious food is served to epicures in an informal mood.
Crystal and gas lights illuminate the entrancing scene, and blackamoors,
as piquant as a French sauce, pose against the lovely view of formal gardens.
A pavillion that takes you back to the French Empire Caribbean . . .
to a royal fête, to a garden party!

La Ronde Bar

To the tinkling of a merry-go-round . . .
you can sit and sip in this transported Parisian sidewalk café,
complete with little potted trees clipped to a French nicety!
Overlooking the La Ronde Room through a wall of glass
open to the magnificent terraces . . . the Fontainebleau's La Ronde bar
overlooks nothing for your pleasure!

hotels, each had its own distinct appeal and style. Ben Novack commissioned Lapidus to design the Fontainebleau, which opened on December 20, 1954, on the site of the old Firestone Estate. In 2005, it closed for major renovations to the tune of $1 billion and reopened in 2008.

In 1954, guests had the following food, drink and entertainment options:

The Poodle Room—cocktail lounge
Boom Boom Room—French-Haitian nightclub offering Calypso beats
Chez Bon Bon—coffee shop
La Ronde—circular supper club; seating capacity for eight hundred
La Ronde Bar—styled after a Parisian sidewalk café; it overlooked La Ronde
Fleur de Lis—classic French restaurant

After reopening in 2008, guests had the following food, drink and entertainment options:

Gotham Steak—steakhouse
Scarpetta—Italian
Hakkasan—Cantonese American
La Côte—two-level poolside bar and grill
Vida—Pan American
Blade Sushi—Japanese
Solo—café and patisserie
Fresh—snacks and gelato
LIV—nightclub, formerly 1954's Tropigala Lounge
Arkadia—lounge
Bleau Bar—bar
Glow Bar—bar

Harry Mufson, who also collaborated on the Fontainebleau project with Ben Novack, later commissioned Lapidus to design the Eden Roc, located adjacent to the Fontainebleau and opened the following season. In food and beverage offerings, it wasn't as expansive as its neighbor. The hotel was home to the Café Pompei, a supper club that offered entertainment with dinner similar to La Ronde (but again, not as grand), as well as the Mona Lisa Room, a formal dining room, and Harry's American Bar. Novack was angry and in retaliation erected a building that cast shade over the Eden Roc's pool. The Eden Roc was also remodeled in 1997 and expanded in 2006. The hotel now houses the renowned 1500 Degrees restaurant. Both hotels experienced a slump in the 1970s due to the expansion of suburban Miami.

THE JEWISH DIASPORA AND THE DELI

Miami's first permanent Jewish settler, Isidor Cohen, arrived on February 6, 1896. Cohen was a prominent pioneer merchant in early Miami. On the mainland, Miami was largely a Jewish community until the 1960s. But on Miami Beach, it was a different story. Up until 1936, Jews were not allowed to buy property on Miami Beach and were highly discriminated along with African Americans. After World War II, Miami Beach became a Jewish vacation spot. There were kosher hotels like the Saxony and delis galore, such as the South Beach, the Uptown, the Villa, the Gourmet Shop and Junior's. In Miami, delis experienced their height of popularity in the 1950s. From Wolfie's to Cohen's Rascal House and Arnie and Richie's, Miami was a deli haven and South Beach a Jewish heaven. "Most of the Jews moving down in the sixties were Eastern European immigrants who had lived in New York," Ira Sheskin wrote. "They didn't mind living in high-rises. To them, South Beach reminded them of New York City."[27] "Miami Beach was Jewish back then—period!" said Arnie London, the former owner of Arnie and Richie's, the last original deli in Miami Beach (it was sold to the Roasters 'n Toasters chain in 2008).[28] According to Sheskin, a demographer at the University of Miami, in 1982, 62 percent of Miami Beach's population was Jewish. This statistic changed drastically in the 1980s, when Miami Beach became dangerous and property prices soared through the roof. Today, there are fewer than seventeen thousand Jewish residents in Miami Beach. This combined with the mass influx of new Latin American residents caused mass flights of the Jewish community to other cities in South Florida, including West Palm Beach and Boca Raton.

The mass flight of the Jewish community deeply hurt the deli community in Miami. In a list of all Jewish delis in David Sax's book, only four were located in Miami: Mo's Bagel and Deli (Aventura), Arnie and Richie's, Bagel Bar East and Bagel Cove. But not even being listed in the *Condé Nast Traveler*'s 50 Best Restaurants in the Country could save Wolfie Cohen's Rascal House. The beloved restaurant suffered a horrible death, as it was bought out by Jerry's Famous Deli Inc., the devil of the delis.

Recently, a deli revival in Miami has been spurred by the one-man army of Josh Marcus—just Josh to the many who trek to Surfside to eat traditional deli fare at his Josh's Deli & Appetizing. This is no boring or stale bagel deli, which has become the most common style of deli to surface in Miami in most recent years. Marcus is running what many have deemed a nouvelle style deli in the heart of Surfside, Miami's Jewish hub, adjacent to a temple and many other delis, both kosher and non-kosher but none as exciting as Josh's. Interestingly enough, many customers walk into the open-format deli inquiring whether or not it is a kosher deli. And while the strict Orthodox Jewish community is dying out, a count of kosher locations in the Miami area tolls at around ninety-three—a significant number, considering that many of these restaurants are present in the Jewish-heavy areas of Miami-Dade County: Surfside, Sunny Isles, North Miami Beach, Aventura, Miami Beach and Bay Harbor Islands.

Food-wise, what have the Jewish folk brought us? Chicken soup with matzo balls, mishmash, cabbage borscht, mushroom barley soup, kishke, knishes, kreplach, rye, challah, pletzl, bagel, hush puppies, chopped liver, gribenes, gefilte fish, coleslaw, latkes, pastrami, corned beef, salami, karnatzel, pickled tongue, rolled beef, Montreal smoked meat, roast brisket, stuffed chicken, smoked turkey, kosher hot dogs, knoblewurst, reubens, flanken, seltzer, Cel-Ray tonic, rugelach, cheesecake, blintzes, stuffed cabbage, cholent, lokshen kugel and black cherry soda. The deli is the Ashkenazi style of Jewish cooking. "So no, New York didn't invent Jewish deli. But New York provided the perfect incubator for the Jewish delicatessen to blossom into a vibrant symbol of Ashkenazi cookery and an outlet for the melding of Jewish food and American culture."[29] In Miami, the concept of the "Jewban" is popular and strong in numbers. Food-wise, it differs from the Ashkenazi style of cooking, which has its origins in Eastern Europe, Germany and France. The Jewbans are usually Sephardic Jews, and their foods are heavily influenced by the Iberian Peninsula, heavier in herbs and spices such as cumin, cilantro, turmeric and cinnamon.

The Great Gables, the "World's Most Beautiful Drive-In Restaurant," was located in Coral Gables. The restaurant was fairly popular in the community and the last of a dying breed. Mel Goldstein, son of the owner, began working there at the age of thirteen as a soda jerk. At this time, the southwest section of Miami was home to a large Jewish community. The restaurant made its own whipped cream and was the second largest Florida carrier of Swiss Premium ice creams. According to Goldstein, the Pizza Palace, Big Wheel, Orange Julep and Red Diamond Inn were also popular during that time. Mel Goldstein noted that Miami's eaters have always been fickle, gravitating to the latest trend, and this is the main reason why many great restaurants sometimes fail. In the 1960s, the Goldstein family opened Pumpernick's in North Miami, along with other restaurants of the same kind. They sold their last restaurant in 1999. The secret to their lasting success? They made fresh food every day. "We treated our customers well and our employees, too," noted Goldstein.[30]

THE 1960S

The 1960s was an important decade for Miami, as a number of events changed the course of the city forever. Miami experienced two waves of immigration from Cuban refugees, once in 1960 and again with the "freedom flight" airlifts. The freedom flights (1965–73) marked the second great wave of Cuban migration to Miami, as "almost 300,000 Cubans arrived in the United States."[31] Simultaneously, as the Cuban refugees came in 1960, President Eisenhower cut imports of Cuban sugar by 700,000 tons, a move that resulted in a drastic increase of production of Florida-grown sugar. The incoming Cubans settled in the area that is now known as Little Havana. A modern-day Ellis Island, a large Jewish community was living in the area upon the arrival of the Cubans, who pushed them out. But before the Cubans and even the Jews, the Bahamians ruled Little Havana. Back then, the area was separated into the Riverside and Shenandoah neighborhoods. In the 1930s, a large number of Jews from the north came and settled in the Shenandoah and Riverside neighborhoods, bringing their businesses with them. The area flourished until the 1950s, when another land boom spurred new communities and developments, and many of the area's residents moved out just in time for the Cubans' arrival.

As a city of the South, Miami was heavily segregated and a hotbed for racial inequality. Two of the most discriminatory downtown locations were McCrory's and the soda fountain at Woolworths. A June 28, 1959 *Miami Herald* story reported that fifty members of the Congress of Racial Equality waited three and a half hours without being served at the Woolworth counter. On the upside, because of desegregation, African American performers no longer had to trek to Overtown for lodging after performances. They could stay at any of the hotels on the island, but it was too little too late. The previously mentioned Booker Terrace Motel continued its importance in the

Map of Little Havana. *Credit: Phillip Ulbrich. Sources: GEBCO, NOAA, National Geographic, DeLorme and Esri.*

Lincoln Road Mall sign.

decade of the 1960s, as it was the location for many of Martin Luther King's press conferences. (It is said that he stayed in Room 51.) Another famous guest of the hotel was boxer Muhammad Ali.

When it opened in 1962, Dadeland was an open-air mall with no food court—very different from the Dadeland of today. Instead, there was the Summit Restaurant and a grocery store, Food Fair. The site of the grocery store is now home to the food court. Summit Restaurant eventually became the Forum, a chain of cafeteria-style restaurants from Missouri. Lincoln Road, another open-air mall, opened in Miami Beach and was designed by the famed Morris Lapidus. On the other side of the county, in Homestead, a little boy with a sign caused pandemonium at Robert Is Here. As a marketing strategy, six-year-old Robert was ordered by his father to stand on the corner of the street and sell cucumbers, surrounded by signs that read "Robert Is Here." Now in its fifty-third year, the fruit stand and market is a can't-miss destination in Homestead. Monty's Raw Bar opened in Coconut Grove at the same time that hippies from all over the country came to invade the neighborhood, making Peacock Park their home and freely eating the fruit from the trees that lined the streets. Popular restaurants included Sorrento's and Red Diamond Inn, both of which served Italian cuisine, the latter being a go-to spot for dates. Lum's was also founded at this time. With its humble beginnings as a hot dog stand in Miami Beach, it grew to be one of the nation's top restaurant chains.

In the 1960s, the use of credit cards became common, and the beach was no longer only for the wealthy. It was also during this decade that Miami Beach began its decline—one that would last until the 1990s. The first half of the 1960s was prosperous, but the onset of the drug culture out of San Francisco in the second half of the decade hurt the seaside hotspot. That cache of the glamorous and gaudy 1950s was no longer relevant, and it would take awhile for that idea to leave people's minds.

Nationally, there was a resurgence in the interest in French cooking due to Julia Child's first book, *Mastering the Art of French Cooking*. The casseroles of the 1950s were out, and complicated food was in. Junk food also became popular, as the decade brought us Tab, Pop-Tarts, Shake and Bake, Doritos and Pringles. The average suburban family patronized family-style restaurant chains such as Howard Johnson and the newly opened Wendy's, and ethnic cuisine continued its rising popularity. In this decade, the national influences didn't pervade as highly as before, mainly due to the growing Cuban population, which instead of assimilating created something completely different than immigrants moving to other parts of the country.

THE 1970S

The '70s saw Alice Waters come onto the scene to reintroduce the notion that would kick off a culinary movement across the entire country—California Cuisine—a return to the land and the importance of utilizing natural and seasonal ingredients. Her mantra? Fresh food, simply prepared. Locally, this would inspire chefs in the next decade with the uprising of the Mango Gang, but before its popularity, another rising was about to change Miami's food landscape forever.

"Yes, mam, this place has surely changed," said sixty-nine-year-old Aubrey Iley, who has been coming to Mae and Dave's for more than thirty-five years. "I remember when I used to 'coon hunt right around the (Hialeah) race track, and out there on 79th Street were the pig farmers." Across from Mae and Dave's, the vacant lot has been replaced by a shopping center, and the names all are Spanish. Like much of the rest of Hialeah, Palm Avenue reflects the influences of its 62 percent Latin population. Businesses once owned by American citizens have been sold to the incoming Cuban exiles.[32] The 1970s was an eventful food decade for Miamians. The phenomenon of the Cuban diaspora is one of immense importance and interest. Now, a decade after the first Cubans had arrived, American restaurants, Italian restaurants and Jewish delis were living harmoniously alongside Cuban restaurants, and that would be the norm from that point on. While initially hopeful, the first immigrants subconsciously knew that they would never go back to Cuba, and this was the guiding strength for their business success. They were scrappy folk and good businessmen, and they quickly took over whatever businesses were left behind by the original inhabitants of their neighborhoods. They knew that they would have to recreate another Cuba here. This group's coming was not like diasporas in other cities, where the groups quietly moved in and assimilated to the area. The Cubans transformed Miami into a more Latin-centric city. In *Cuban Miami*, Robert Levine and Moisés Asis note:

> *Menus of Cuban restaurants and cafeterias in Miami today might include café con leche (Cuban coffee with milk); sandwiches made on toasted, buttered Cuban bread (lighter and more airy than its French counterpart) with ham, roast pork, cheese, and pickles; fritas (spicy thin hamburgers with onions); Cuban-style rice and black beans; cream cheese and guava pastries; and tropical fruit shakes. Once considered exotic, Cuban food today is a staple for Miamians of every background.*[33]

Exterior of Versailles Restaurant.

It was difficult for those Miami residents that wanted nothing to do with the Latin community to escape its influence—and even more difficult to escape its food. The most important Cuban restaurants of the '70s included Badia's and Versailles. Badia's, a local favorite, was popular for its cheap meals and was known for having the best *palomilla* in town. Versailles is a gargantuan palace, offering a full restaurant of 350 seats, two *ventanillas*, and a walk-up coffee window that serves more than one thousand *cafecitos* a day. Versailles was opened by Felipe Valls, whose family has long been an important part of the community, owning not only the famous restaurant but also eight La Carreta restaurants and the upscale Spanish mainstay Casa Juancho on Calle Ocho. Versailles is named after an eatery of the same name in Havana.

The success of the Cubans in the last decade influenced the rise of immigration from other Latin American countries, specifically from Central America, where the instability of governments grew by the day. Hondurans,

Nicaraguans and Salvadorans from Central America and Argentines from South America trickled in by the thousands in the 1970s and '80s. Just as powerful as the Cubans, Nicaraguans have also had a lasting imprint on the city. The largest number of Nicaraguans can be found in Sweetwater (aka "Little Managua"), but *fritangas* (the name for restaurants that serve authentic inexpensive Nicaraguan fare) can be found throughout the entire city. The Nicaraguan staples are more universal and palate pleasing, favorites even amongst non-Latin communities.

Aside from the Latin influences, there was a large emergence and subsequent rise in popularity of chain and fast-food restaurants, mainly due to the large suburban flights. As Miami grew in population, it also grew in size. Residents, no longer wanting to live in downtown, began to move into and expand the residential suburban communities of Miami, and the downtown area began to die. This marked the beginning of the end for mom-and-pop shops.

French and Italian foods also made a comeback during the 1970s. In 1978, *Miami Herald* restaurant critic Philippe De Vosjoli reported, "Last year, there was a 32 percent increase in the number of Italian restaurants in this country."[34] Miami followed suit, and De Vosjoli pointed out the following as favorites: Raimondo's, Marcella's My Kitchen, Pappagallo and Casa Santino.

The most notable restaurants of the decade included Christine Lee's Gaslight at the Golden Strand Motel in North Beach; Café Chauveron on Bay Harbor Island (most popular dishes included the pate of wild duck, roasted quails, Pergordin pheasant, soufflé and chocolate mousse); Raimondo; Le Festival in Coral Gables; Janos in Hialeah; Garcia's Seafood Grille & Fish Market; and People's Bar-B-Q, of which the last two still exist today.

Ribs also gained popularity during this decade, and a *Miami Herald* article from 1978 detailed the top places to eat, which included, Bar-Be-Que King, Big Al's Bar-B-Que, Culpepper's Plantation Pit Bar-B-Q, Flynn's Dixie Ribs, New Hickory Barbeque, Ole Hickory, Pit Bar-B-Q, Roy's Georgia Barbecue, Shorty's Bar-B-Que Ranch and Uncle Tom's Barbecue. Tony Roma's, known for its ribs, had its beginning here, too. In the 1980s, Roma would sell the restaurant to a company that would turn it into the worldwide chain that it is now. In the 1990s, antsy to get back into the restaurant world, he opened Tony's Pelican Harbor Restaurant, a seafood restaurant that did not fair very well. His claim to fame really was his ribs.

Chapter 6

1980s AND BEYOND

THE 1980s

Nationally in the 1980s, the food scene was decadent. David Leite of Leite's Culinaria notes:

> *Think early 1980s and certain images come to mind: the Reagans draped in designer clothes, Trump's gaudy towers, and, most horrific, oversize restaurant plates cradling an infinitesimally small amount of food. Nouvelle Cuisine, as it was coined in the late '70s in France, was the hottest thing here. Diners now paid astronomically more to eat significantly less, and loved it. It was a sign of status to wait a half hour for a table, eat a pigeon's portion of food, and then be the first to foist a platinum credit card on the waiter, loudly declaiming to the table, "This one's on me!" The stock market was everyone's best friend, and generosity flowed. But soon diners rebelled and instead opted for plates filled with sumptuous delights. At home, we collected all types of gourmet foods and gadgets. Cabinets overflowed with $65 bottles of virgin olive oil and 50-year-old balsamic vinegars. Countertops were cleared to make way for the new stand mixer and the food processor. And drawers fairly bulged with the newest culinary gizmos, the result of reverent pilgrimages to the Mecca of cooking, Williams-Sonoma. This was also the time when many chefs stepped out from behind their stoves and found celebrity. Wolfgang Puck became a household name as his*

Paella being cooked during Hispanic Heritage Week at the Miami-Dade Community College's Mitchell Wolfson New World Center Campus in 1984. The paella included 650 pounds of rice with thousands of pounds of chicken, rabbit and duck. *Courtesy of the State Archives of Florida, Florida Memory Project.*

InterContinental Miami's chef Marshall Burke and food and beverage director Tim Herman at President Reagan's dinner reception in 1986. *Photograph by Murry Sill,* Miami Daily News, *1986.*

much-touted gourmet pizzas attracted the new Hollywood glitterati to his restaurant, Spago. At the same time, manufacturers found ways to make everything reduced fat, low-fat or fat-free—even fat. What foodie can forget where he was when he heard that Olestra, the new nonfat fat, was on its way to market? But try as we might, most of us didn't lose weight. We fooled ourselves into believing that because we were eating low-fat foods we could guiltlessly binge.[35]

Locally, Miami was in a state of transition. Downtown Miami was still suffering from the suburban flight and expansion. Miami Beach was a strange mix of old folks sitting on rocking chairs waiting to die along with cocaine smugglers and a dangerous class of newly imported immigrants from Cuba. The third wave of the latter, most commonly known as the Mariel Boatlift of 1980, sent over 150,000 immigrants that were different from the first two waves of Cubans—these newcomers were poor, and a large amount of them were criminals. In 1981, the unstable government of Haiti also sent hoards of refugees to Miami's lands. But immigration policies had changed, and the Haitians were not as warmly received as the first two waves of Cuban immigrants, and racial tensions caused a slew of riots and discrimination in this decade. Haitian immigrants moved into the area called Little Haiti, located just north of today's Design District.

Another important community at the height of the 1980s was Kendall, as it served as one of the new suburban frontiers. Migration into Kendall began in the late 1970s but skyrocketed in the 1980s. One of its first food proprietors was Jimmy Schweitzer, who owned a pizza parlor in Westchester that served as the closest restaurant for Kendallites. "There were no restaurants in West Kendall," recalls Saul Sack, who moved to Kendale Lakes in 1973. "We had to drive to Bird Road or into the Gables. Times sure have changed. When Schweitzer began tossing and baking pizzas back in 1970, West Kendall folks could buy hot buttered corn from roadside vendors and pick strawberries, but they had to travel miles to buy a bagel or even a burger."[36] Another restaurant popular in the 1980s in Kendall was Toby's Bar and Grill in the old Town and Country shopping center, which catered to the more affluent crowd. Kendall was the new frontier because it provided luxury, prosperity and status for those people that had moved out of Little Havana.

The most popular restaurants of the decade included Veronique's, inside of the Biscayne Bay Marriott Hotel and Marina; Regine's at the Coconut Grove Grand Bay Hotel, a continuation of Café Chauveron; Casa Juancho; the Dining Galleries; El Sevilla; Il Tulipano; the Grand Café; La Scala; Le

Festival; the Miami Palm; the Pavillon Grill; the Spoonbill; Tiberio; Vinton's; Tanino's; Siam Lotus; Mandarin Garden; Max's Place; Madrid Restaurant; Buccione; JJ's Diner; Café Fedora; Charade Restaurant; Toby's Bar and Grill; and Christine Lee's Gaslight, which began as a Chinese restaurant and then turned Continental, offering some of the best steak in town. The Gaslight changed menus over the years to appeal to a larger crowd of people and changed locations several times from its original home in the Golden Strand to the Thunderbird and then RK Plaza. One of the most notable food stories from this era is when President Reagan stopped into Little Havana's La Esquina de Tejas while in Miami. He ate a meal of chicken, rice and beans, plantains, flan and café Cubano.

Bayside Marketplace opened in the later part of the decade, and with it came a slew of new restaurants, including Las Tapas, owned by Felipe Valls of Versailles; Peacock Café; and Savannah Smiles, along with a full-fledged food court offering everything from hot dogs to Bahamian food and a raw bar. Now the marketplace is filled with chain restaurants such as Bubba Gump Shrimp, Chili's, Hooters, Hard Rock Café, The Knife and local favorite Los Ranchos. In sad news, Pumpernick's in North Miami shut down after twenty-seven years of business. Also, Casa Larios in South Miami witnessed the opening of Daniel's, one of Miami's first openly gay dining spots and lounge, in 1987.

One of the most famous hotels of the decade was the Mutiny Hotel. Opened in the late 1960s but hitting its peak in the drug-laced years of the 1980s, the Mutiny Hotel was known for lavish decadence, extreme partying and good cocaine. It was a nonstop party, hosting an assorted clientele from the most honorable to the most criminal, including Jackie O., George H.W. Bush, drug dealers, politicians, Madonna, dictators, gunrunners and undercover DEA agents. How grand was this place? The whole decadence of South Beach would never even come close what was going on at this hotel. Aside from the partying, it was an important hub for the CIA, as some of the most important deals and undercover stings were conducted there.

Inspired by the California cuisine of Alice Waters in the 1970s, the second half of the 1980s forever changed the track of Miami's food. The Mango Gang appeared and set in motion a series of events that would again change the way Miamians ate and viewed food. The imprint of the Mango Gang began in 1986 with the opening of Chef Allen Susser's restaurant Chef Allen's in Aventura, and the food world rejoiced. Who else was part of the Mango Gang? Norman Van Aken, Douglas Rodriguez, Mark Militello and, to a lesser extent, Dewey LoSasso, Pascal Oudin and Robin Haas. The

MANGO SALSA

Note: Cucumber adds crunch to this summery mango salsa. When peeling the cucumber, I like to leave a few strips of dark green skin in place for extra color. If you are leaving the skin on, wash the cuke with hot water to remove any wax coating. If mangos are unavailable, the salsa could be made with peaches. This salsa goes well with grilled meats and fish of all sorts. It's also a great vegetable side dish.

Ingredients:
2 cups diced ripe mango
1 cucumber, peeled, seeded and diced
½ poblano chili, seeded and minced
1 jalapeno chili, seeded and minced
2 teaspoons minced fresh ginger
¼ cup chopped fresh mint or cilantro leaves
1 tablespoon packed light brown sugar, or to taste
¼ cup fresh lime juice
Salt and freshly ground black pepper, to taste

Preparation:
Combine all of the ingredients in a mixing bowl, and gently toss to mix. Correct the seasonings, adding salt, lime juice or sugar to taste. The salsa should be a little sweet and a little sour. Mango salsa tastes best served a couple of hours after making. Refrigerate covered until serving.

From Steven Raichlen's *Miami Spice*.

Mango Gang is credited with creating a new genre of cooking called New World Cuisine or Nuevo Latino or Floribbean, a blend of Latin, Caribbean, Asian and American flavors. The Mango Gang got its name from the frequent use of the mango fruit in its recipes. Examples of popular recipes include grill-roasted rack of lamb in red mole, xinxim (chicken and seafood stew with coconut milk and nuts), tiradito of scallops, avocado and pistachio-crusted gulf snapper with black-bean sauce and ruby grapefruit and shallot and cilantro mojo. *Miami New Times* writer Lee Klein noted, "Just as Alice Waters prodded Californians to take notice of locally produced products such as gorgeous goat cheese and orgasmic organic foods, these mango fellas ripened awareness of the tropical fruits and vegetables in our own backyards, as well as the stellar seafood abundant in our waters."[37] It was a return to the land, using fresh, local ingredients and mixing them in a way that was different than before. In 1987, Doug Rodriguez began as the chef at Wet Paint Café on Lincoln Road. In 1988, Mark Militello opened Mark's Place in North Miami. And finally, in 1989, Douglas Rodriguez opened Yuca in Coral Gables and Norman opened A Mano in the Betsy Ross Hotel. The movement evolved quickly, and the following decade was when it got interesting.

THE 1990S

The following quote from Lee Klein in 2012 perfectly summarizes Miami dining in the 1990s:

> *To enter Bianca, the Delano Hotel restaurant that arrived at January's end, is to step back in time to South Beach during the heady '90s. In those days, fine-dining establishments could charge what they wanted for whatever fussed-up fusion cuisine they felt like serving. They could provide negligent service and give off the sort of pretentious, condescending attitude for which SoBe came to be known.*[38]

Not to say that nothing good came out of the decade, but overall, the 1990s were a strange time in Miami's food scene, and every chef has a different opinion about its importance or non-importance. The movement that began in the last years of the 1980s continued with fervent following through the mid-1990s and served as a platform on which future chefs would emerge. Many of today's popular chefs worked and learned under these heads. There did come a point after the mid-1990s where Miami's food scene became stagnant. The Mango Gang had reached the end of the line, and a lot of the up-and-coming chefs in the former part of the decade left to learn from other great chefs, leaving Miami's food scene with little to be desired and few innovators to take it to the next level.

People were also going away from the overly gaudy times of the 1980s, and there was an ~~emphasis on weight loss and fusion cuisine, while~~ the concept of the food celebrity emerged with the premiere of the Food Network in 1993. Here's an interesting side note:

Before the success of the Food Network and the onslaught of what follows, aspiring foodies relied on the food sections of their location newspapers for their gastronomical fix. These sections, thick with grocery store advertisements in the 1950s and 1960s, originated in the women's pages—narrowly defined at the fashion and household pages—of metropolitan dailies across the country. Then as now, food sections reflected gender roles, health standards and governmental policies about food in a community. They also reflected the developing demographic of many cities as new immigrants settled into communities and shared their dishes. Lastly, these sections related stories about food—creating a form of culinary anthropology, as Jeanne Voltz, the former Los Angeles Times food editor, once described her work.[39]

Voltz became what one culinary authority described as "the best-known food expert you've probably never heard of." She headed the *Miami Herald* food section in the 1950s.

In the 1990s, culinary movements were tracked more heavily, and chefs gained celebrity status. Food gossip columns emerged in both the *Miami Herald* and the *Miami New Times*, which regaled their readers with the stories of Andrea Curto and Frank Randazzo (at the time, Andrea was at Wish and Frank at the Gaucho Room) or the various celebrities that loved to traipse around many of the South Beach hotels like Cameron Diaz's Bambu, opened under the helm of Karim Masri. The 1990s was a playground for celebrities in Miami, and dining turned into a "see and be seen" event rather than a simple epicurean delight.

The key players during the decade, in no particular order, included Pascal Oudin, Robin Haas, Kerry Simon, Jonathan Eismann, Carmen Gonzalez, Michael Schwartz, Hedy Goldsmith, Kris Wessel, Phillipe Ruiz, Jan Jorgensen, Cindy Hutson, Michelle Bernstein, Andrea Curto-Randazzo, Jeffrey Wolfe, Ken Lyon, Willis Loughead and Johnny V. Many of the aforementioned, of course, are even more renowned today and are continuing the teaching platforms for the new chefs to emerge in the coming years. Many of these chefs learned under the Mango Gang masters. The most popular restaurants of the '90s included Blue Star, Starfish, Max's, Crystal Café, the Colony Bistro (in 1994, this was the hottest spot in Miami),

Bang, Baleen, Red Square (an extremely popular Russian restaurant, a first of its kind), Red Fish Grill, Liaison, Two Chefs, Norman's, Ortanique on the Mile, Pacific Time, Nemo's, Perricone's, Tantra and Wish.

The opening of Wish, the high-end eatery inside of the newly remodeled Tiffany Hotel, caused a stir, as its menu did not offer meat. Chef Kerry Simon and Johnny V were favorites of both diners and critics and developed fervent followings. They are best known for frequent restaurant flipping and hopping. Johnny V worked under Norman at A Mano and Kerry Simon at the Raleigh's Blue Star. Simon was often referred to as the "Caribbean Cowboy," as his signature style merged New World Cuisine with Southwest cookery. Jonathan Eismann and Ken Lyon both took risky chances with the openings of their restaurants, Pacific Time and Frères et Compagnie, on the then-dead Lincoln Road. The Grand Café at the Grand Bay Hotel was one of the best in town, along with Palme d'Or, headed by Paul Oudin. Back to the Mango Gang, Doug Rodriguez moved to New York to spread his Nuevo Latino concept, while Norman left A Mano and reappeared with the opening of Norman's in 1995. Mark closed Mark's Place in 1997. In 1999, the Oak Room and the Pavilion Grill closed to make way for the $4 million Indigo Restaurant at the InterContinental Miami.

Most notably, in 1994, a chef by the name of Michael Schwartz opened a mini restaurant empire (including Nemo, Big Pink and Shoji Sushi) in the South of Fifth neighborhood in Miami Beach with Myles Chefetz. Hedy Goldsmith was the pastry chef for the restaurants. The partnership eventually dissolved, but it set the table for what was to come in the 2000s.

All in all, the 1990s was a strange decade for local chefs. It served as a transitional period in which ideas were tested, chefs honed their skills and the ones who didn't belong left, all making way for one of the most interesting and vibrant food revolutions of the new decade.

THE 2000S

A quote from Sam Gorenstein right after his James Beard Award nomination in 2010 neatly sums up the previous decade's stagnation:

> *In Miami, the gastronomic scene is not the same as in New York or Chicago. Big chefs that were leading the pack in Miami never developed their sous chefs*

or chefs de cuisines. They didn't nurture the new wave. Laurent has opened eighteen restaurants in the company, and he makes sure he develops his chefs de cuisines. Then, those chefs will open their own places one day. This never happened in Miami. New talent was never developed, and the dining scene got stuck. Restaurants were more centralized in seeing how they could extract more money out of the tourists rather than putting the best product out there. That's changing now. Michelle Bernstein and Michael Schwartz are doing a great job with this. New talent is finally being nurtured.

Predating social media, the quest for celebrity superstardom was already in effect. As quoted in an interview with Jen Karetnick, Norman Van Aken says the following of young chefs: "These days, young chefs are mesmerized by fame and whether or not they're in the papers. They think they're not succeeding if they're not in *Food Arts* this week."

In the 2000s, the key players included Tim Andriola of Timo Restaurant & Bar. A Mango Gang University alum, Andriola worked under both Chef Allen and Chef Militello. Josh Marcus of Josh's Deli also did stints at La Sandwicherie, North One 10 and China Grill before opening Chowdown Grill. Michelle Bernstein hopped from Red Fish Grill to Tantra to The Strand before heading to Azul and finally opening Michy's in 2006 in the then–highly segregated MiMo neighborhood. The Strand hotel's restaurant, not be confused with Gary Farmer's original 1980s Washington Avenue restaurant of the same name, also launched an interest in food.

In 2003, the JW Marriott launched a Chef of the Month program that invited South Florida CEOs into the kitchen of Isabela's, its fine-dining restaurant, to cook a three-course meal with the chef. 2004 experienced the decline of the pastry chef, and in an interview with Lee Klein, Michelle Bernstein stated that the famed Sra. Martinez was almost called Rincon Cuarenta or Buena Vista.

The most popular restaurants of the decade included Barton G., Escopazzo, the River Oyster Bar, Michael's Genuine, Michy's, Palme d'Or, Prime One Twelve, Nobu, Sardinia and Red Light. Norman made his triumphant return in 2002 with the opening of Mundo at the Village of Merrick Park. Dewey opened North One 10 in 2004 as a pioneer of the Biscayne Corridor. Whole Foods premiered its first store in South Florida in Coral Gables in 2007. The 2000s also continued the celebrity interest with Emeril's at the Loew's Hotel, Table 8 and Bouley.

The South Beach Wine & Food Festival premiered in 2001, although it really dates back to 1997, when it was a one-day fundraising festival at

Chef Norman Van Aken. *Courtesy of Norman Van Aken.*

Florida International University called Florida Extravaganza. The event has grown to over ten thousand attendees and includes events costing more than $200 a piece. Miami Spice debuted in 2002. Barton G. opened in the old Gatti's and Bluestar space. Remember Food Café by Lorena Garcia? It was one of the first restaurants in the Design District. Now, Garcia appears on Taco Bell commercials. Doug Rodriguez's flip flopping was as much his signature as his Latin cuisine. In 2003, OLA began on 5061 Biscayne Boulevard. It then moved to Coral Gables, and a second outpost was added to the Savoy Hotel. The Coral Gables location closed, and the beach spot moved from the Savoy to the Sanctuary. Ironically, the first location is now the corporate offices for Barton G. The area of MiMo is now hot—he should've stuck it out.

Two restaurants that opened too soon were Sheba Ethiopian Restaurant in the Design District and Urbanite Bistro in Lower Wynwood/Arts and Entertainment District. Sheba closed in December 2008, and we no longer have the option for that kind of food. Prior to Sheba were A Taste of Ethiopia and Kafa Café, which also tried but failed. Opened for less than a year, Urbanite Bistro was infusing rarely used ingredients in strange, new and exciting forms and also hosting beer dinners. Its menu featured a "tastings" section, which included items such as alligator egg rolls with mango-roasted jalapeno cream. Entrees emphasized game and seasonal produce and included roasted boar tenderloin (with purple sticky rice and grilled broccoli rabé); ancho-glazed grouper (with cucumber salsa, blue cornbread, sautéed broccoli and malanga); and organic roasted poussin (with challah stuffing, seasonal vegetable succotash and papaya-rum marmalade).

One of the more cutting-edge restaurants of the time, La Broche, took a cue from Ferran Adria and dabbled in molecular gastronomy—again too early for its time. Angel Palacio's restaurant lasted less than a year. Chef Jordi Valles cooked at La Broche and then took the helm of Mosaico, which opened in the same location in 2004. All located in the Firehouse Four Building, Mosaico was upstairs, while Salero and La Tienda were downstairs. Salero was a casual café, and La Tienda was a Spanish food/wine retail shop. But it all came crumbling down in 2007. The building, originally the first firehouse in Miami, now houses Sushi Maki and DOLORES but you can call me LOLITA.

In the last section, I told you about Michael Schwartz's breakup with Myles Chefetz. Schwartz came back strong with the opening of Michael's Genuine in the heart of the Design District in 2007, propelling the Miami scene into the international spotlight and bringing Hedy Goldsmith with him. Inspired by Schwartz, Jonathan Eismann and Ken Lyon moved their restaurants to the Design District as well—Eismann moving Pacific Time and Lyon opening a brand-new restaurant called Fratelli Lyon. Down the street, in Midtown, Sugarcane Raw Bar & Grill opened in 2009. Sugarcane was headed by Chef Timon Balloo, who was also a Mango Gang alum, having worked under Chef Allen along with Michy at Azul and Kris at Elia. He also did a stint at Domo Japones, which eventually became home to Sra. Martinez.

Sustain opened in December 2010 under executive chef Alejandro Pinero, who previously worked under Michelle Bernstein at The Strand and was also chef de cuisine at Fratelli Lyon with Brian Goldberg and familiar local face Aniece Meinhold. Meinhold would go on to open Phuc Yea!, the city's first pop-up restaurant, and the mini restaurant empire Pious Pig, consisting of Acme Bakery and The Federal.

One cannot talk about Miami cuisine without mentioning Kris Wessel, a pioneer for promoting true Florida cuisine. Wessel has been in the scene since the early 1990s, working as chef de cuisine at Mark's Place before moving on to open Liaison on Espanola Way. In 2008, the MiMo neighborhood was still not gentrified, even though Michelle had set off a small boom in 2006 with the opening of Michy's. But that didn't stop customers from going to the small restaurant inside of Motel Blu. Red Light was a neighborhood gem, finally shuttering in mid-October 2012. At first, the close was temporary, as the chef was preparing for the opening of his new restaurant, Florida Cookery, but alas, he never returned due to an eviction notice from the landlord on October 24, and die-hard Red Lighters never had a chance to bid farewell to their beloved restaurant. Wessel's signature barbecue shrimp dish was birthed in 2000 at Liaison, where the trend of growing your own herbs and making bread and ice cream from scratch was already being done. Wessel poignantly sums up Miami's cuisine at the time:

We were the cracker side of Florida culture, but there were these other cultures that arrived—influences from South America, the Caribbean, New York. That's what really makes up Miami Beach. If you exclude any of those, you're not representing everything that South Florida is, was, and will be. Despite the name, it's not a drive towards…a cracker approach to the food. (Laughs). My view of the cultural and ethnic influences on Miami is the whole region. What influenced Miami over the years, from the 1930s until now? Well, South America influences Miami, the American South influences Miami, the Caribbean influences Miami…and New York City influences Miami—in the way Mark (Militelo), Norman (Van Aken) and Allen (Susser) would take Florida products in the nineties and emulate how they treated product in big restaurants in New York and nationwide. I think they got caught up with the press in New York and California…but if you ignore South America, the Caribbean, and the American South…you have to have at least two or three dishes that have the flavor of each (of those) on your menu, or you're not giving a regional interpretation of Miami or Florida. I mean, nowadays, when the season opens up in October, you can get wild boar right outside of Lake Okeechobee. You can get frog legs north of Jupiter. So, I think gone are the days where you just have to use stone crabs and key lime pies to represent Florida and Miami.[40]

The decade of the 2000s was also one of trial and error, but the latter years breathed life into the stagnant scene. Now, new chefs like Sam Gorenstein, Bradley Herron, Giorgio Rapicavoli and Jeff McInnis, along with mixologists Robert Ferrara, Gabriel Orta and Elad Zvi, are creatively and quickly changing the beat of Miami's food. Miami's food world has seen more change and excitement in the last three years than it has during any of the previous decades. It's an exciting time to eat in Miami.

MIAMI BLOGS

According to *Saveur*, food blogs originated in 1997 with Chowhound. Growing in popularity over the years, they initially began as places to share personal stories and adventures in cooking and baking. More recently, they have become masterpieces and serious business, featuring great writing that spans all forms of food topics—some even gaining James Beard Awards.

Local favorites like Frodnesor and Chowfather have been active in the forum space since the early 2000s. Miami's own food-blog scene is equally amazing and ever growing, starting off slow and steady in 2005 and hitting its peak in 2012. As of 2013, there are approximately eighty-five active food blogs in the city. Our first official food blog was Sara Liss's *All Purpose Dark*, as her first post was published on September 14, 2005. The national aggregate blog *Eater* finally made its way to Miami in 2009 and was instantly received with open arms, with local gossip columnist Lesley Abravanel at the helm.

Following is the blog's inaugural post:

OCTOBER 20, 2009:
We may be the southernmost foreclosure capital in the country, but that doesn't mean foodies have to resort to spam and caviar just yet. To beat the banking blues, several of the city's swankiest eateries have issued their own version of a pricing detente. To wit:

The China Grill Empire: Blue Door and Asia de Cuba have agreed to extend their Miami Spice prix fixe menus through Halloween, while China Grill and Kobe Club will offer the $35 three-course dinners and $22 three-course lunches through November 30.

Hot off her Top Chef guest judge appearance, chef Michelle Bernstein offers a $22 lunchtime (M-F noon-3 p.m.) prix fixe menu of two small plates, one large plate and one dessert at SRA. Martinez called Bueno, Bonito Y Barato. Translation? "Good, Pretty and Cheap."

On Wednesdays at Talula, Buon Appetito features a bottomless bowl of rigatoni with chef/owner Andrea Curto-Randazzo's special Sunday Sauce along with meatballs, salad, garlic rolls and espresso panna cotta for $29 per person.

JAMES BEARD FOUNDATION AWARDS

The rat race to gain traction in the food world became even greater with the introduction of the James Beard Foundation Awards in 1991. In the more recent years of the 2000s, Miami has seen a large number of nominations and even some winners. But during the earlier years of the awards, we only received a few mentions. Miami was first put on the map in 1994 when Chef Allen Susser received the James Beard Award for Best Chef Southeast. We would not receive another mention again until 2004, when Michelle Bernstein was nominated for Best Chef Southeast. Following is a full list of all Miami James Beard Award nominees, semi-finalists and winners throughout the foundation's history. As you'll see, it's a great indicator as to the strength and rise in popularity food-wise that the city has gained over the years.

1994
Best Chef Southeast: Winner
Allen Susser; Chef Allen's

2004
Best Chef Southeast: Nominee
Michelle Bernstein; Azul

2007
Best Chef South: Nominee
Michelle Bernstein; Michy's

Best Chef South: Nominee
Jonathan Eismann; Pacific Time

2008
Outstanding Restaurateur: Semifinalist
Laurent Tourondel; BLT Restaurants

Best Chef South: Winner
Michelle Bernstein; Michy's

Best Chef South: Nominee
Douglas Rodriguez; OLA

Best Chef South: Semifinalist
Philippe Ruiz; Palme d'Or

Outstanding Chef: Semifinalist
Allen Susser; Chef Allen's

Outstanding Service: Semifinalist
Palme d'Or, Biltmore

Best New Restaurant: Semifinalist
Michael's Genuine Food and Drink

2009
Best Chef South: Nominee
Michael Schwartz; Michael's Genuine Food and Drink

Best Chef South: Nominee and Semifinalist
Douglas Rodriguez; OLA

2010
Best Chef South: Winner
Michael Schwartz; Michael's Genuine Food and Drink

Best Chef South: Semifinalist
Kris Wessel; Red Light

Best New Restaurant: Semifinalist
Eos at Viceroy

Outstanding Pastry Chef: Semifinalist
Hedy Goldsmith; Michael's Genuine Food and Drink

Rising Star Chef of the Year: Semifinalist
Sam Gorenstein; BLT

2011
Best New Restaurant: Semifinalist
Sugarcane Raw Bar & Grill

Rising Star Chef of the Year: Semifinalist
Sam Gorenstein; BLT

Outstanding Restaurateur: Semifinalist
Myles Chefetz; Myles Restaurant Group (Prime One Twelve, Prime
Italian, Shoji Sushi, Nemo, Big Pink)

2012
Outstanding Pastry Chef: Nominee and Semifinalist
Hedy Goldsmith; Michael's Genuine Food and Drink

Top: Chef Kris Wessel of Florida Cookery.

Middle: Pig's head at a local butcher shop.

Bottom: Sushi pairing seminar at the 2012 South Beach Wine & Food Festival. *Courtesy of Seth Browarnik, World Red Eye.*

Top: Chef Michelle Bernstein at the 2012 South Beach Wine & Food Festival. *Courtesy of South Beach Wine & Food Festival.*

Middle: Chef Ingrid Hoffman at the 2012 South Beach Wine & Food Festival. *Courtesy of South Beach Wine & Food Festival.*

Bottom: Scene at the Redland Farmers' Market.

Top: Cuban coffee street window in Little Havana.

Middle: Jewban sandwich at Josh's Delicatessen & Appetizing in Surfside.

Bottom: Produce at Robert Is Here Fruit Stand and Farm in Homestead.

Top: Frita Cubana at El Rey De Las Fritas on Calle Ocho in Little Havana.

Middle: Yardbird Southern Table & Bar's fried chicken. *Courtesy of David Cabrera.*

Bottom: Michelle Bernstein's Korean fried chicken. *Courtesy of Andres Aravena.*

Top: Exterior of Lime Fresh Mexican Grill.

Middle: Lime Fresh Mexican Grill tacos.

Bottom: My Ceviche's mixed ceviche. *Courtesy of Andres Aravena.*

Top: A plate at the Biltmore Hotel. *Courtesy of the Biltmore Hotel.*

Middle: Chef Douglas Rodriguez's modern take on *arroz con frijoles* with pork belly. *Courtesy of Andres Aravena.*

Bottom: Yardbird Southern Table & Bar's macaroni and cheese. *Courtesy of David Cabrera.*

Top: FIU students from the Chaplin School of Hospitality and Tourism Management. *Courtesy of Mitchell Zachs, MagicalPhotos.com.*

Middle: Chef Michael Moran and student from the Chaplin School of Hospitality and Tourism Management. *Courtesy of Mitchell Zachs, MagicalPhotos.com.*

Bottom: Chinese bok choy.

Top: Jerk chicken on the barbecue.

Middle: South Florida boasts an up-and-coming honey production industry.

Second from bottom: Stone-crab claws.

Bottom: Orange grove in Homestead.

Best New Restaurant: Semifinalist
Yardbird Southern Table & Bar

Rising Star Chef of the Year: Semifinalist
Jarrod Verbiack; DB Bistro Moderne

Best Chef South: Semifinalist
Paula DaSilva; 1500 Degrees

Best Chef South: Semifinalist
Jeff McInnis; Yardbird Southern Table & Bar

Best Chef South: Semifinalist
Sergio Navarro; Pubbelly

2013
Best Chef South: Nominee and Semifinalist
Jeff McInnis; Yardbird Southern Table & Bar

Best Chef South: Semifinalist
Jose Mendin, Pubbelly

Best New Restaurant: Semifinalist
Khong River House

Outstanding Bar Program: Semifinalist
Broken Shaker

Outstanding Pastry Chef: Nominee
Hedy Goldsmith; Michael's Genuine Food and Drink

Rising Star Chef of the Year: Semifinalist
Giorgio Rapicavoli; Eating House

In another category titled "America's Classics," the foundation honors legendary family-owned restaurants, and Miami claims three: Joe's Stone Crab received the honor in 1998, Versailles Restaurant received the honor in 2001 and Jumbo's Restaurant received the honor in 2008.

Chapter 7

DAIRIES, SUPERMARKETS, FAST-FOOD RESTAURANTS AND A BAKERY

DAIRIES

It's always important to note the era of European exploration when speaking about food. Christopher Columbus's expeditions set into motion the change in how we eat today and the transference of food and traditions. For the first time, the Old World and New World were connected. Ponce de Leon first brought cattle to Florida in 1521, but it would be years before there was enough dry land to support herds of beef or dairy cattle in South Florida. The descendants of these cows, Cracker Cows, eventually adapted to the climate of the area and developed immunities to many of the area's parasites and bacteria.

The early farming settlers to the Miami area took advantage of the fruitful land and indeed used most of the land available for farming. Miami was a large dairy producer, and the whole area that today is known as the city of Miami Springs was originally dairy farms.

Dr. John G. Dupuis Sr. founded the White Belt Dairy with Dutch Royal White Belt cattle. The dairy was located four miles west of Lemon City on the West Little River. At the height of the dairy, 500,000 gallons of ice cream and milk were distributed annually in the area. Puritan Dairy was created in 1934 and located on 160 NE Thirtieth Street but met its demise in August 1960, when a price war for milk broke out and stores could no longer stock it.

Cows in pasture.

Dressel's Dairy was extremely popular in the 1960s, and it owned a dairy bar that served milkshakes, ice cream and sundaes. It also delivered milk and other dairy products to customers around the county. Dressel's Dairy was originally Milam Dairy, which purchased it from R.A. Milam in 1941. The popular Milam Dairy Road in Miami Springs is named after Mr. R.A. Milam. The Dressels eventually sold the dairy to McArthur Dairy (owned by Dean Foods since 1980), which is still in operation today and now widely distributed throughout the larger South Florida region—from West Palm Beach to the Florida Keys. The McArthur Dairy family has its roots in the early beginnings of dairy farming circa 1929—not in the city limits of Miami but a little farther north in Hollywood.

Supermarkets

In the supermarket world of Miami, three top dogs take the lead: Publix, Winn-Dixie and Sedano's. In more recent years, there has been an increased interest in mom-and-pop stores and organic foods, and a large number of specialty food stores such as Whole Foods, Fresh Market, Gardener's Market, Milams and Epicure have opened. The popularity of cheaper, ethnic specialty markets, including the Asian markets and Presidente Supermarket, has also increased.

In the early beginnings of Miami, prior to the mid-1940s, mom-and-pop supermarkets ruled. And it's interesting to note that in the first years of the city's existence, supermarkets were more like commissaries, selling a variety of items. Much of the food that was consumed during that time was still produced on farms and by families for personal use. The earliest grocery stores in Miami (in sequential opening order) belonged to E.L. Brady, J.E. Lummus and T.N. Gautier. Opened in April 1896 immediately after Brady's arrival in Miami, E.L. Brady and Company was the leading grocer in the city. This is the originating site of the December 1896 fire that burned down three blocks of businesses. After that year's Christmas celebrations, a firework got lodged under the wooden-framed store and eventually went off in the early morning hours, giving little chance for residents to react. Not much could have been done anyway, as Miami did not have a firefighting system at the time.

Two of the most popular supermarkets in the 1940s and '50s were Shell's Superstore and Steven's Supermarket. In this era, there was a large boom to the area, and nationally, there was an increased interest in cooking. These two chains ended up making enormous headlines in their day. According to a February 11, 1948 *Miami Daily News* article, Shell's Superstore, located on 5941 NW Seventh Avenue, opened as the largest grocery and meat store in the world, stretching two city blocks. Some fun facts about this Shell's store: the bakery turned out 15,360 donuts daily, and the vegetable counter stretched seventy-five feet. Another article in the May 15, 1955 issue of the *Miami Daily News* reported that Steven's Supermarket, now the largest outlet in the country, opened in South Miami on the corner of Red Road and Dixie Highway, the current location of the popular Sunset Place shopping mall. Steven's was a local chain of supermarkets that had humble beginnings as a country store on NW Twenty-seventh Avenue and 58 Street. At its peak, the chain amassed nine stores. The aforementioned store had enough parking

The E.L. Brady grocery store. *Courtesy of the State Archives of Florida, Florida Memory Project.*

for 538 cars. Scores of shoppers actually followed behind others into the parking lot and helped them load groceries into their cars so that they could claim their carts. Extra police enforcement was also hired—and in good judgment, as a mob scene even broke out on at least one occasion. The Grand Union Company purchased the Steven's company in the early 1960s.

We've seen other large chains come and go, including Food Fair, Piggly Wiggly (1920s Coral Gables and 1930s downtown Miami), XMart and Albertson's. Winn-Dixie also has its beginnings here with Mrs. Ethel Chase Davis. In November 1925, Ethel and her husband began their first Table Supply Store at 5905 NE Second Avenue. The chain eventually grew to 519 stores in eleven southern states. The Table Supply Store was originally Rockmoor Grocery in Lemon City and was renamed. Its headquarters eventually left the city, but its origins were here. As the company grew, it purchased more supermarket companies, and the Winn-Dixie name did not come about until 1955.

Publix, most synonymous with Miami food shoppers, does not have origins in South Florida but in Central Florida. The first Publix to open in Miami was in 1959, and more recently, the first Sabor Publix debuted in Hialeah in an effort to appeal to the ever-expanding number of Latin Americans in

Exterior of Sedano's Supermarket in Hialeah.

Gilda crackers at Sedano's Supermarket.

Florida. Sedano's also has its roots in Hialeah with Armando Guerra, an ex-patriot of Cuba, in 1962. In 1971, Guerra brought Manuel Herrán on board to help out with the daily operations of his small business. From its humble beginnings, Sedano's is now the number-one Hispanic retailer in the nation, with thirty-four supermarkets across South and Central Florida. Herrán's son currently runs the show.

FAST-FOOD RESTAURANTS

The most famous fast-food chains to come out of Miami are Royal Castle, Burger King and Pollo Tropical. Royal Castle, Miami's first foray into fast food, opened in 1938 and was "fit for a king." Founded by William Singer, the restaurants were modeled after the nationally popular White Castle. The economic state of the country led to the large popularity of fast-food restaurants. While extremely popular, White Castle went out of business in 1976, not able to compete against the big dogs of McDonald's and Burger King. Two Royal Castle locations with different owners still exist—Wayne Arnold owns the location at 12490 NW Seventh Avenue, while James Brimberry owns the location at 2700 NW Seventy-ninth Street. The latter is the more famous of the two, as James Brimberry held a stake in the restaurant. After the Civil Rights act of 1964, Brimberry was hired as the first black manager for the brand. The restaurants were in full effect during the Civil Rights movements of the 1960s but did not allow black customers to sit at the counter, instead forcing them to order items through a side window.

Burger King came onto the scene in 1954 on 550 Brickell Avenue (in the heart of the now bustling financial district of Brickell) as Insta Burger King. Partners Jim McLamore and Dave Edgerton propelled it into the prosperous fast-food chain that it is today. Pollo Tropical began with humble roots and a simple recipe for citrus-marinated grilled chicken in 1988 on 741 NW Thirty-seventh Avenue. Its main goal was to share the signature food of Miami's tropical tastes. Do you remember when Pollo Tropical won the Super Bowl of black beans and rice? According to the company's website, "Created as part of the pre-game events leading up to the 1999 NFL Super Bowl in Miami, Pollo Tropical established a Guinness World Record for the largest serving of black beans and rice. The bowl was 10 feet in diameter, and the serving size weighed more than 3,000 pounds."

Royal Castle advertisement in the December 3, 1956 issue of *Miami News*.

Here's a surprising fact: While Miami Subs Grill carries the Miami moniker, its roots do not lie in Miami but in the Keys, where it was originally called Mr. Submarine. Even more shocking are recent rebranding efforts, which include a partnership with Miami singer Pitbull and a "new" name: New Miami Subs Grill. The company hopes to reclaim the fame of the 1980s, when it was at the peak of its popularity. It is also the only fast casual restaurant to have Dom Pérignon on the menu, which pairs well with its signature Philly cheesesteak.

HOLSUM BAKERY

Before Sunset Place and the horribly mapped-out Bakery Centre, Holsum Bakery stood on South Dixie Highway and Red Road. Originally built as a movie theater, the bakery took over the site in 1934 and ran the operation in the same location well until the 1980s. The bakery was started by Charles and Annie Fuchs, immigrants from Germany who purchased Homestead Bakery and Meat Market and changed the name to Fuchs Baking Company in 1931. "When the family company became affiliated with the Long Foundation of Food Research of Chicago in 1933, Fuchs began using 'Holsum,' a Long trademark, on its bread wrappers. W.E. Long Company grew to be the largest cooperative of independent bakers in the United States, and its members still use the Holsum name on bread products sold throughout the country."[41] The bakery has deep roots in Miami and is one of the community's best immigration success stories. In 1994, Fuchs Baking Company was sold to Interstate Baking Company, one of the country's food empires.

Chapter 8

RECIPES AND OTHER FINDS

In looking through countless Miami cookbooks, I found the number to be in the hundreds. The following is a compilation of the strangest recipes encountered. As they are listed in chronological order, you will notice the culinary transformation that has taken place in Miami over the years.

St. Patrick's Parent-Teachers Association Cookbook (1931)

An interesting inscription found in the first pages of this cookbook serves as a friendly reminder to women of their necessary role in the kitchen:

500 Ways To Please a Husband

We may live without poetry, music and art,
We may live without conscience, and live without heart.
We may live without friends, we may live without books,
But civilized man cannot live without cooks.
—Owen Meredith

PIAVE SALAD

Ingredients:
I cup lunch tongue
I apple
Lettuce

Salad Dressing
I green pepper, minced
I canned pimiento, minced

Preparation:
Arrange the lettuce on individual plates, lay on it two or more slices of tongue. Peel, core and slice the apple crosswise, place a slice on each portion of tongue. Pour a spoonful salad dressing over and sprinkle with minced green pepper and pimiento.

SEA FOAM

Ingredients and Preparation:
2 cups brown sugar, I cup water. White of I egg beaten stiff on large platter. Let sugar and water boil until it forms a hard ball in cold water. Pour syrup slowly into white of egg, stirring constantly. Before it gets too stiff, a lb. pecans, make into small balls when cool enough with a teaspoon and fingers.—Mrs. A.L. Fahnestock.

What else does it take to feed a man? Other recipes that can be found in the cookbook include: citrus cocktail, lime juice cocktail, afternoon tea, fruit juice punch, corn meal muffin, golden tea biscuits, bran muffins, nut bread, sour cream waffles, gingerbread, cheese soufflés, shrimp creole, baked egg, poached egg, clam chowder, creamed cod fish, oyster stew, salmon loaf, bouillon, asparagus soup, mutton broth, cream of mushroom soup, meatballs, chicken a la king, baked ham in blanket, chop suey, pork chops, lima beans, potato croquettes, buttered beets, fried okra, corn fritters, macaroni salad, date pudding, fig pudding, papaya sherbet, custard, Boston cream pie, lemon pie, pumpkin pie, pecan pie, date bars, deviled ham sandwich filling and mango marmalade.

Cross Creek Cookery (1942)
By Marjorie Kinnan Rawlings

JELLIED TONGUE (POTAGE DIXIE)—LUNCHEON DISH

Ingredients:
1 small or medium-sized fresh beef tongue
1 stalk celery
1 slice of onion
2 bay leaves
6 whole cloves
6 whole allspice
2 tablespoons vinegar
1 teaspoon salt
1 cup to 1 can beef consommé
1 tablespoon gelatin
3 to 5 hard-boiled eggs
1 tablespoon Worcestershire sauce

Preparation:
Boil tongue slowly in cold water to cover well, adding all the seasonings except Worcestershire. When tender, in two to two and one-half hours, turn out fire and let tongue cool in the broth. Peel tongue and cut out any small bones or coarse particles at the thick end. Cut in slices lengthwise and put through the meat grinder. Put the hard-boiled eggs through the meat grinder. Mix with the ground tongue. The number of eggs and the amount of consommé depend on the size of the tongue. Soak gelatin in two tablespoons of the cold consommé. Heat the rest of the consommé to boiling and pour over the gelatin, stirring until dissolved. Mix with the ground tongue and eggs. Add Worcestershire and more salt to taste. Turn into a mould. Set in icebox to harden. Serve on a platter of lettuce leaves or grape leaves, and pass a generous bowl of tart mayonnaise.

BEAR STEAK

Bear Meat. Bears, once so plentiful in Florida that before 1792 William Bartram wrote, "There are still far too many bears in Florida," are becoming scarce. I see no reason for destroying the remaining ones, since they live so far from any domestic clearing that they are no longer a menace, as formerly, to stock. But I must admit that bear meat at the proper season, and properly cooked, is delicious meat.

Preparation:
Hang rib steaks of bear as long as possible without spoiling. Brush with salt and pepper and melted bear fat or olive oil. Broil over hot live oak coals about twenty minutes, turning twice. Serve with baked sweet potatoes and coleslaw.

MAYHAW JELLY

Ingredients:
1 pound mayhaws (ripe but not soft)
1 pound sugar
1 quart water

Preparation:
Wash mayhaws and boil with the water until tender, about twenty minutes. Strain through a jelly bag. Place juice in a kettle, bring to a boil, and add sugar slowly, stirring. Let boil until jelling point is reached. I first had this delicate rosy-pink jelly on a bear hunt near the St. Jon's River. A big burly Cracker six feet tall had brought it along, of his wife's making, as his contribution to our food on the hunt.

The Miami Woman's Club Cookbook (1954)

PINEAPPLE-CHEESE SALAD
BY MRS. HARRY L. DOBBS

Ingredients:
1 package lemon jello
1 pinch salt
1 cup boiling water
Cool until set, then add:
½ pound cottage cheese or Philadelphia cream cheese
½ pint whipped cream
1 small can crushed pineapple

Preparation:
Add dressing to which you have added 1 tablespoon cream.

Members of Redland Woman's Society of Christian Service (1956)

DEVILED DIP
BY MRS. M.E. WILSON

Ingredients and Preparation:
Scoop meat from ½ large ripe avocado, leaving shell intact. Mash avocado meat, blend in 1 family-size can deviled ham, 1 3-oz. cake cream cheese, minced parsley and seasoning, to taste. Mix smooth and pile in reserved shell. Served surrounded with crisp fresh vegetable pieces, potato chips, small crackers.

CARISSA CREAM BY MRS. ROBERT NEWCOMB

Ingredients:
1 tablespoon gelatin
½ cup cold water
1 cup boiling Carissa juice
½ cup sugar
1/16 teaspoon salt
1 cup heavy cream, whipped

Preparation:
Soak gelatin in cold water 5 minutes, dissolve in boiling Carissa juice and add sugar and salt. Stir until sugar dissolves, then chill until slightly thickened. Fold in whipped cream and chill until firm. Un-mold and serve as dessert.

Other recipes found in book include, green tomato pickle, sweet pickled grapefruit rinds, chayote relish, cream of tomato soup, turkey supreme with celery sauce, crawfish enchilada, papaya shortcake, lime chiffon pie, sweet spiced loquats, calamondin marmalade, green tomato mincemeat and sweet potato balls.

Political Pot Luck (1959)
By Meg Madigan

University of Miami Office of the President
Jay F.W. Pearson, President

TURKEY BARBECUE WITH AVOCADO

Ingredients:
1 10–15 pound fresh or frozen turkey
1 fairly ripe avocado

Preparation:
Put ¾ avocado through ricer. Stuff unseasoned avocado pulp between ribs only in body cavity of the turkey—adding a sprinkling of Parmesan cheese if desired. Before stuffing cavity, sprinkle inside with approximately two tablespoons salt. Truss turkey and tie firmly onto spit, balancing carefully.

Make form aluminum foil a rectangular tray to collect drippings and place under turkey. Make a fire of briquettes well clear of turkey and tray. Prepare sauce as follows:

Ingredients:
½ cup Wesson or other vegetable oil
½ teaspoon salt
½ teaspoon coarse ground black pepper
½ teaspoon Accent
*½ teaspoon Hickory smoke salt
¼ teaspoon each powdered Rosemary, onion salt, celery seed, paprika
Juice of one lime

Preparation:
Mix thoroughly and brush on turkey as it barbecues, allowing 15–20 minutes per pound, depending on weather and appearance of turkey. Do not be concerned if avocado stuffing drips into tray.

Simmer neck and giblets until very tender, remove from bones and grind the meat. Add remainder of diced avocado to drippings from turkey (and half of the ground giblets if desired). Add all to broth in which giblets were cooked. To make gravy, thicken this mixture with flour and water to proper consistency and add salt to taste, if needed.

Note:
*If a strong wind is blowing during barbecue, charcoal salt is not needed! If larger turkey is used, increase ingredients.

South Florida Cookery (1964)
By Alex D. Hawkes

CHICKEN COCONUT GROVE

Serving size: 4

Ingredients:
4 fresh semi-ripe coconuts
3 cups canned chicken a la king
¼ cup sherry
½ cup coconut water
⅛ teaspoon Cayenne pepper
2 teaspoons minced chives
4 thick slices Cuban or French bread
3 tablespoons flour

Preparation:
Puncture the "eyes" of the coconuts, draining off all the water (or "milk," as it is usually incorrectly called), reserving this. Saw through the coconuts to make cups with lids near their tops. Meanwhile, combine the chicken a la king, sherry, coconut water (do not use all of it!), Cayenne pepper and chives. Spoon this mixture into the coconut shells. Mix the flour with a little warm water to form a smooth paste. Put some of the paste around the edge of the coconut shells and seal the tops on them. Bake the sealed coconuts in a 325 degree Fahrenheit oven for about 3 hours. Toast the bread slices until crisp, scoop out centers to form holders for coconuts, and serve, allowing yours guests to unseal them.

Westminster Ladies Guild Cook Book (1966)

DRIED BEEF DIP—MRS. J.M. VROON SAMPLER'S DELIGHT

Ingredients:

I large 8-ounce cream
   cheese
I pkg. dried beef
I tablespoon horseradish

I can tomato sauce
   (family size)
I pkg. dried onion
   soup

Preparation:
Mix together.

Other recipes found in the book include coleslaw, meatballs, pork chops, dumplings, walnut orange rolls, coconut frosting, shrimp salad, green bean casserole and paella.

The Florida Cookbook (1973)
By George S. Fichter

TURTLE STEAKS

Ingredients:

2 pounds turtle steaks
⅛ teaspoon thyme
¼ teaspoon pepper
¼ cup olive oil

I can cream of
   mushroom soup
¼ cup flour
I teaspoon salt

Preparation:
Steaks should be cut across the grain of the meat and then pounded thin with a steak mallet or the back of a cleaver. Sprinkle pounded steaks with salt, pepper, thyme, and flour. Fry in oil until browned on both sides. Add mushroom soup (thinned and smoothed with water) and simmer for about 20 minutes. Serves 3–4.

Best of the Best from Florida: Selected Recipes from Florida's Favorite Cookbooks (1986)
Edited by Gwen McKee and Barbara Moseley

FLORIDA SUNSHINE SALAD

Ingredients:
1 3-ounce package lemon gelatin
1 12-ounce can apricot nectar
1 6-ounce can frozen orange juice, thawed
1 3-ounce package cream cheese
½ cup pecans

Preparation:
Heat apricot nectar to boiling point. Dissolve lemon gelatin in this. Do not dilute. Add can of orange juice undiluted. Make small balls of the cream cheese to which pecans have been added, and place 3 small balls in each mold. Fill mold with juice mixture and refrigerate until jellied. This is good with fowl, pork or ham. It may also be used at holiday time in place of cranberry sauce. It can be made in one large mold or 6 individuals molds. We prefer to use the individual molds.

NOODLE CROQUETTES

Serving size:
Makes about 18–24 croquettes

Ingredients:
½ pound thin noodles
4 tablespoons butter
3 tablespoons flour
1 cup cream
1 egg

1 yolk
½ teaspoon salt
¼ teaspoon pepper
⅔ cup grated cheddar cheese
½ cup grated Parmesan cheese
2 eggs
2 tablespoons water
2 tablespoons Oil
½ teaspoon salt
2 cups flour
2 cups bread crumbs
1 cup clarified butter for frying*
   (2–3 ¼ pound sticks of butter or margarine)

Preparation:
Cook noodles as directed on the package. Drain well. Melt butter in a saucepan, add flour and cook 2–3 minutes, stirring constantly. Add cream, stir and cook 1 minute. Beat in egg and yolk and add salt, pepper and cheese. Add the noodles. Simmer, stirring constantly until very thick. Cool completely, then refrigerate for 1–2 hours or overnight. Beat together eggs, water, oil and salt. Scoop up the noodles with a spoon and shape into round balls. Roll into flour, then dip into egg and roll in the crumbs. Fry until golden brown in the clarified butter. Keep warm and serve.

*Clarified Butter: To clarify margarine or butter, melt in a small pot. Let stand for 10 minutes, remove the white sediment on top, and pour off the golden liquid. Throw away the white residue which formed on the bottom. This butter will keep for 2–3 weeks in the refrigerator. Keep in a jar with a tight lid.

Biscayne Bights and Breezes: A Cookbook with Loving Memories of Miami (1987)
By Villagers, Inc.

COCOANUT PUDDING

Heat one quart of milk, then add three tablespoonfuls of sugar and one half cup grated or shredded cocoanut and one teaspoonful butter. Then add four tablespoonfuls of Florida arrowroot starch, previously mixed with a little cold milk, then stir constantly until well thickened and creamy.

GUAVA PUDDING

Prepare guavas as for canning and stew until tender; sweeten to taste. Put in pudding dish or agate pan and cover with a batter of one cupful of flour, three quarters of sugar, one cupful of milk, one egg, one teaspoonful of baking powder, and one tablespoonful of melted butter, added last. Bake in moderate oven about half an hour.

Coffee was in short supply and very expensive for the pioneers of the South Florida coast. One substitute was derived from the plentiful sweet potatoes. They were cut into small pieces and baked until charred. The charred chunks were then ground in a coffee mill and brewed like regular coffee. Served piping hot, the drink certainly had the same look as coffee, but the taste was said to be somewhat like Poslum.

Famous Florida Recipes: 300 Years of Good Eating (1997)
By Lowis Carlton

FLORIDA GREEN ICE CREAM

Ingredients:
1 medium avocado, de-seeded and mashed (¼ cup of pulp)
⅔ cup sugar
3½ tablespoons lime juice
1 cup pineapple juice
½ teaspoon salt
1½ cups light cream

Preparation:
Stir all ingredients together until thoroughly blended. Freeze in ice cube tray until almost firm. Break up and whip until light and fluffy. Turn into fancy 1-quart mold and re-freeze 2 hours or until firm. Makes 6 servings.

JFK SALAD DRESSING (CREATED BY FONTAINEBLEAU HOTEL CHEF AT MIAMI BEACH FOR JOHN F. KENNEDY)

Ingredients:
5 whole eggs
1 clove garlic
1 teaspooon salt
¼ teaspoon pepper
2 tablespoons paprika
1 teaspoon
  prepared mustard
3 cups salad oil
1 cup olive oil
½ cup red wine vinegar

Preparation:
Crack eggs into bowl. Crush garlic and add. Combine with salt, pepper, paprika and mustard; mix well. Add oils slowly, beating constantly. If mixture gets too thick, add a little vinegar. Continue beating; add all of the vinegar until thoroughly blended. Add salt and pepper to taste.

Exotic Foods: A Kitchen and Garden Guide (2002)
By Marian Van Atta

TROPICAL CATSUP

Ingredients:

4 pounds prepared guavas
1 quart vinegar
2 pounds sugar
1½ pounds raisins
1 pound preserved ginger

1 teaspoon salt
1 clove garlic
2 tablespoons hot peppers
¼ cup each, white
    mustard and celery seed

Preparation:

Cut blossom and stem ends from fruit peel if blemished and remove seed. Grind in food chopper with raisins, garlic, ginger, mustard seed and peppers. Add remaining ingredients and boil 30 minutes. Let stand overnight. Reheat, bottle and seal. Allow to season several weeks before using.

BANANAS WITH CHEESE

Ingredients:

½ pound American cheese
6 to 8 bananas
½ cup breadcrumbs
2 tablespoons butter

Preparation:

Fill a buttered baking dish with alternating layers of bananas (cut crosswise) and grated American cheese. Cover the top with buttered breadcrumbs. Place cover on dish and bake slowly at 325 degrees Fahrenheit for about one hour. Remove cover and allow crumbs to brown. This is an excellent luncheon dish when served with a green salad.

ROSELLE JAM

Ingredients:
2 pounds prepared calyces
1½ cups water
Juice and rind of 1 lemon
Sugar

Preparation:
Add water, lemon juice and finely cut lemon rind to calyces and cook until soft. Measure and add an equal amount of sugar. Return to fire and cook slowly until of jam consistency (about 20 minutes). Pour into hot sterilized glasses and seal with paraffin.

In the early days of cookery, simple cookbooks were essential for the transference of important and now-common cooking information. Basic things that we now take for granted were not the norm back in the earlier days. Two great books that aided in this knowledge transference were 1914's *Florida Salads* and 1944's *Florida Seafood Cookery*. Each dealt with very specialized and narrow topics but got into the nitty gritty of it all. *Florida Salads* taught about the importance of eating salads, its benefits and enjoyment, how to pick leaves and other tips, like how pineapple aids in digestion. Following are two simple recipes that can be found in the book:

CHEESE AND GREEN PEA SALAD

Cut American cheese in tiny little blocks and mix with green peas, which have been cooked and drained. Sprinkle with white wine pepper, lightly fold in mayonnaise and serve on lettuce.

FLORIDA PECAN SANDWICHES

Grind the meat of Florida pecans, scrape or grate firm apples, mix all with mayonnaise and spread on thin slices of white bread.

Other recipes that can be found in *Florida Salads* include Florida fruit dressing, lemon jelly, mayonnaise, potato dressing, asparagus salad, cauliflower salad, salad croquettes, celery salad, chicken aspic salad, kumquat salad, mango salad, pomelo salad and chicken salad loaf.

Menu Suggestions

Menu suggestions were still popular in 1987. Following are plenty of menu suggestions from the Guild of the Museum of Science's *Make It Miami* cookbook. Naturally, this guide is presented at the end of the book, and recipes for all of the suggested dish items are available within the book.

BON VOYAGE BRUNCH

Florida Summer Punch
Scrambled Eggs
Ham Broccoli Roll-Ups
Hot Curried Fruit
Citrus Lime Muffins
Best-Ever Mango Bread
Strawberry Butter

LADIES LITE LUNCHEON

Pool-Party Mint Tea Punch
Microwave Strawberry Soup Supreme
Crab and Shrimp Quick
Toasted Fingers
Mango Mousse

"ORANGE" BOWL DINNER

Orange Cow
Chutney Fingers
Salad Mandarin
Miami Orange Chicken
Orange Rice
Orange Fluff Cake
Florida Orange Pie

CARIBBEAN CUISINE

Trinidad Rum Punch
Conch Fritters
Wine-Gelatin Ring
Coconut Shrimp
Caribbean Pigeon Peas and Rice
Grapefruit Alaska

ELEGANT DINNER

Champagne Punch
Bleu Cheese Mousse
Caviar Pie
Almond Soup
Brandied Roast Cornish Hens with Peaches
Green Bean Salad Provencal
Baby Pilaf
Chocolate Mousse Cake

CINCO DE MAYO MEXICAN FIESTA

Jim's Sangria
Microwave Burrito Tidbits
Party Tapatia
Mango Salad
Chalupas
Chicken Enchilada Ole
Cheese Casserole Squares
Spanish Flan

POOLSIDE BARBECUE

Miami Moonlight Cocktail
Dilly Shrimp Dip with Crackers
Tricolor Salad
Barbecued Dolphin
Tartar Sauce
Bleu Cheese Potato Casserole
Herb-Dressed Italian Bread
Key Lime Pie

SOUTHERN AMERICAN POTPOURRI

Yellow Birds
Ceviche
Guatemalan Stuffed Tomatoes
Cuban Boliche Roast
Spanish Rice Casserole
Cubano Buñuelos
Tres Leches

SOUTHERN SUPPER

Iced Tea Drink
Chicken and Dumplings
Southern Green Beans
Southern-Style Creamed Corn
Honey Buttered Carrots
Strawberry Pie

DOCKSIDE PICNIC

Windsurfer's Passion Fruit Quencher
Leek Soup Cheese Ball with Crackers
Chicken Curry Salad
Tomato Pie
Cranberry Relish
Pecan Pick-Ups

SEAFOOD DINNER

Calypso Cup
Pate of Smoked Salmon with Chives and Dill
Gazpacho
Snapper Parmesan
Spinach Topped Tomatoes
Rice with Mushrooms and Almonds
Aerobics Drop-Out Cake

HOLIDAY SEASON DINNER

Cranberry Eggnog
Smoked Oyster Dip with Crackers
Mushroom Strudel
Wild Rice Soup
Orange-Mincemeat Congealed Salad
Roast Turkey with Giblet Gravy
Sicilian Broccoli
Creamed Onions
Sweet Potato Casserole
Brandied Cranberries
Refrigerator Rolls
Old Cutler Holiday Cake
Old English Plum Pudding

CONCLUSION

When you tell people you're writing a food book, they automatically assume that it's a cookbook or a restaurant dining guide. This book was neither. Yes, recipes were included, but they served as teaching tools—examples to provide depth to the historical data. It's fascinating to think that things like sassafras jelly or pineapple cheese were cutting edge at one point in time. As I previously mentioned, there are literally hundreds of Miami/South Florida/Florida cookbooks—many even sprouting as early as the first settlers arrived. Although some of the more rare or out-of-print books are not easily available for purchase, they can still be viewed or checked out (depending on whether they are "Reference Only") at the library or the HistoryMiami archives. Early settlers had the task of finding out what was edible and what wasn't—what worked and what didn't. It was also their task to teach others about this new information and to create recipes that concurred with the eating trends of the time. This is fully evident in the early books, which place an emphasis on local ingredients and provide recipes that are simple and fresh. As the years went on, with the rise in the popularity of ethnic food, more books with immigrant recipes arose.

The beauty of food is that you can make it your own, and that is why it continues to evolve every day. Food is in constant motion. Twenty years from now, when someone finds this book in the library, they will laugh and say, "My, how old-fashioned they were." Just like our Mango Gang forefathers spackled fish with mango salsa, our latest trend of mixing Latin American food with Italian will be a thing of absurdity. This book has shown you where we came from and where we are now—a glimpse into our past, present and future. Again, the thing to remember is that visiting Little Havana will not make your food trip to Miami complete, as it is but one piece of the giant melting-pot puzzle.

Critics of the Miami food landscape say that it is not ethnically diverse enough—that it is too Latin heavy. While that may be true, the Latin and Asian options available are diverse in their offerings, and the development of our palates will only encourage it to be even more open and allow for more ethnic opportunities to bloom. Our palates have finally begun to evolve, and we are now understanding what real food should taste like and seeking out the authentic. We are more educated food-wise. Foods will have less salt or sugar to fit our more evolved palates. The owners of the ill-fated Sheba must be rolling in their "food graves." Open Sheba now, and it would be a sensation—not to be confused with sensationalism. As a community, we are craving that sort of ethnicity to come forth. In *Mmmmiami*, Kotin and Martin note:

> *Miami has always been a city of immigrants and adventurers, culinary and otherwise. In the late 1800s, settlers bartered with the Seminole Indians for wild turkey and venison, kept sea turtles in cages near the water's edge for eggs and meat, and turned guavas and Surinam cherries into preserves. Scavenging was another source of sustenance, some of it surprisingly sophisticated. In 1896, the year the city was incorporated, a menu at the Hotel Miami hinted at cutting-edge things to come with dishes such as sea bass chowder, pineapple fritters, and Indian pudding with wine sauce. The cultural mix that is so much a part of Miami has been here from the beginning, too. The 1950 residents counted in the 1900 census of the city hailed from thirty of the forty-five states, as well as Great Britain, Germany, Sweden, Italy, Russia, Spain, Canada, the Bahamas, and China. A wild land boom in the 1920s, a major Jewish migration from the Northeast in the 1930s, a wave of World War II veterans from the Midwest in the 1940 and '50s, and floods of refugees from strife-torn Cuba, Central America, and Haiti in the 1960s, '70s, and '80s have remade the face of Miami again and again.*

In present-day Miami, there is a culinary revolution afoot—one that is so fervent with followers that it cannot be ignored. What we are experiencing now can be compared to the time of the Mango Gang in that it is a catalyst. The present culinary pioneers are the byproducts of the Mango Gang. It is but the tip of the iceberg, and what's to come food-wise—if continued

Dinner table setup from a Miami dinner. *Courtesy of Justin Namon.*

and carried out correctly—will forever change Miami's eating landscape. In twenty years, someone else will have to document this new era of Miami food. I encourage you to seek out and document your own food adventures in Miami. Happy eating!

ENDNOTES

INTRODUCTION

1. Scott P. Cunningham, "Miami, Florida," *Poets and Writers*, November 4, 2011.
2. Grad, "Memories of Happy Times."
3. Collins, "Remembering Junior's, Corky's and the Roney Pub."
4. Heike Greenwood, "Miami Stories," HistoryMiami, http://www. historymiami.org/research-miami/make-miami-history-now/miami-stories/details/heike-greenwood.
5. Loretta Barish Morris, "Miami Stories," HistoryMiami, http://www. historymiami.org/research-miami/make-miami-history-now/miami-stories/details/loretta-barish-morris.
6. Annita Dewitt Middleton, "Miami Stories," HistoryMiami, http://www. historymiami.org/research-miami/make-miami-history-now/miami-stories/details/annita-dewitt-middleton.
7. Gina Lee Rice Guilford, "Miami Stories," HistoryMiami, http://www. historymiami.org/research-miami/make-miami-history-now/miami-stories/details/gina-lee-rice-guilford.
8. Michael Pearlman, "Miami Stories," HistoryMiami, http://www. historymiami.org/research-miami/make-miami-history-now/miami-stories/details/michael-pearlman.

Chapter 1

9. Florida Department of Agriculture and Consumer Services, http://www. freshfromflorida.com.
10. Sokolov, *Why We Eat What We Eat.*
11. Perennial Solutions, http://www.perennialsolutions.org.
12. FLA-Guide.info, "Fare of Florida Food," http://fla-guide.info/food.
13. Sokolov, *Why We Eat What We Eat,* 55.
14. Mormino, *Land of Sunshine,* 195.

Chapter 3

15. Grunwald, *The Swamp,* 17.
16. Muir, *Miami, U.S.A.,* 5.
17. Ibid., 92.
18. Tomb, "Lemon City Once Lively Community."

Chapter 4

19. Williams, "From Barbecue Shacks to the Mayfair Grill," 22.
20. Armbruster, *Life and Times of Miami Beach,* 91.
21. Ibid., 73.
22. Ling, *Run the Rum In,* 38.
23. Ibid., 34.
24. Baker, *The Gentleman's Companion,* 19.

Chapter 5

25. Mormino, *Land of Sunshine,* 283.
26. Ibid., 285.
27. Carlos Miller "The Jewish Impact on Miami Beach," *Miami Beach 411* (blog), September 10, 2009. http://www.miamibeach411.com/news/jewish-impact.

28. Sax, *Save the Deli*, 178.
29. Ibid., 23.
30. Mel Goldstein, interview with Mandy Baca, February 1, 2013.
31. Mormino, *Land of Sunshine*, 286.
32. Silva, "Along Hialeah's Palm Ave."
34. De Vosjoli, "A Little Italy in Florida."

CHAPTER 6

35. Leite, "Dining Through the Decades."
36. Singer, "Restaurants Try to Satisfy the Kendall Appetite."
37. Klein, "What's the Matter with Miami?"
38. Klein, "Bianca at the Delano."
39. Voss, "Food Journalism," 67.
40. Doss, "Kris Wessel," *Miami New Times* blog, September 21, 2012.

CHAPTER 7

41. Matkov, *Miami's Historic Neighborhoods*, 178.

BIBLIOGRAPHY

INDIVIDUALS

A special thank-you to Roselaine Blenaime, Susan Brustman, Felipe Cuevas, Laine Doss, Raley Ewing, Paul S. George, Mel Goldstein, Sef Gonzalez, Alisah Jeffries, Lee Klein, John Kunkel, Ernesto Lopez, Joshua Marcus, Corinna J. Moebius, JennyLee Molina, Gary R. Mormino, Galena Mosovich, Justin Namon, Paulina Naranjo, Alejandro Ortiz, David Rosendorf, John Shipley, Dylan Terry, Norman Van Aken, Aurelia Vasquez and Kris Wessel for the great assistance throughout this journey.

BOOKS

Altschul, B.J. *Cracker Cookin' and Other Favorites: Cookbook and Restaurant Guide to Florida's Best Eateries*. Altamonte Springs, FL: Winner Enterprises, 1984.

Antón, Alex, and Roger E. Hernández. *Cubans in America: A Vibrant History of a People in Exile*. New York: Kensington Books, 2002.

Armbruster, Ann. *The Life and Times of Miami Beach*. New York: A.A. Knopf, 1995.

Baker, Charles, Jr. *The Gentleman's Companion*. New York: Derrydale Press, 1939.

Brandon, Pam, Katie Farmand, Heather J. McPherson and Gary Bogdon. *Field to Feast: Recipes Celebrating Florida Farmers, Chefs, and Artisans*. Gainesville: University Press of Florida, 2012.

Brown, Sandi. *Famous Florida!: Restaurants and Recipes*. St. Petersburg, FL: LaFray Publishing Co, 1981.

Bucuvalas, Tina, Peggy A. Bulger and Stetson Kennedy. *South Florida Folklife*. Jackson: University Press of Mississippi, 1994.

Carlton, Lowis. *Famous Florida Recipes: 300 Years of Good Eating*. St. Petersburg, FL: Great Outdoors Publishing Co., 1972.

Coachman, Jessie Candler. *Mrs. Coachman's Florida Recipes*. Clearwater, FL: Kumquat Sweet Shop, 1938.

Cowett, Betty Ann. *The Ransom Everglades Guide to an Educated Palate*. Miami, FL: Ransom Everglades School, 1986.

Dickson, Felice. *Growing Food in South Florida*. Miami, FL: Banyan Books, 1975.

Federal Writers' Project. *Florida Seafood Cookery: Tasty and Economical Recipes for the Preparation of Fish, Crabs, Oysters, Shrimp, Clams, Crawfish, Scallops and Sea Turtles*. Tallahassee, FL: Florida Department of Agriculture, 1944.

Fichter, George S. *The Florida Cookbook*. Miami, FL: E.A. Seemann, 1973.

First Presbyterian Church of Miami. *The Florida Tropical Cook Book*. Chicago: Printed by E.F. Harman & Co., 1912.

George, Paul S. *Little Havana*. Charleston, SC: Arcadia, 2006.

———. *Roddey Burdine: His Family and Their Namesake Store.* Hialeah, FL: Fort Dallas Press, 2010.

Grunwald, Michael. *The Swamp: The Everglades, Florida, and the Politics of Paradise.* New York: Simon & Schuster, 2007.

Guild of the Museum of Science (Miami). *Make It Miami: A Cookbook.* Miami, FL: The Guild, 1987.

Harris, Frances Barber. *Florida Salads: A Collection of Dainty, Wholesome Salad Recipes That Will Appeal to the Most Fastidious.* Jacksonville, FL: Jacksonville Printing Co., 1918.

Hauck-Lawson, Annie, and Jonathan Deutsch. *Gastropolis: Food and New York City.* New York: Columbia University Press, 2009.

Hawkes, Alex D. *South Florida Cookery: Unique Recipes from the Tropics and Elsewhere.* Coral Gables, FL: Wake-Brook House, 1964.

Key to Our Kitchen. *Florida Cookery.* Miami, FL, 1900.

Klein, Barbara Seldin. *Dining In: A Collection of Gourmet Recipes for Complete Meals from the Miami Area's Finest Restaurants.* Seattle: Peanut Butter Pub, 1985.

Kleinberg, Howard. *Miami: The Way We Were.* Surfside, FL: Surfside Publications, 1989.

Kotkin, Carole, and Kathy Martin. *Mmmmiami: Tempting Tropical Tastes for Home Cooks Everywhere.* New York: Henry Holt, 1998.

Levine, Robert M., and Moisés Asís. *Cuban Miami.* New Brunswick, NJ: Rutgers University Press, 2000.

Ling, Sally J. *Run the Rum In: South Florida During Prohibition.* Charleston, SC: The History Press, 2007.

Madigan, Meg. *Political Potluck.* Tallahassee, FL: Peninsular Publishing Co., 1959.

Matkov, Becky. *Miami's Historic Neighborhoods: A History of Community*. San Antonio, TX: Historical Publishing Network, 2001.

McKee, Gwen, and Barbara Moseley. *Best of the Best from Florida: Selected Recipes from Florida's Favorite Cookbooks*. Brandon, MS: Quail Ridge Press, 1986.

Miami Woman's Club. *The Miami Woman's Club Cookbook*. Miami, 1954.

Muir, Helen. *The Biltmore: Beacon for Miami*. Miami, FL: Valiant Press, 1998.

Nenes, Michael F. *American Regional Cuisine*. Hoboken, NJ: J. Wiley, 2007.

Parks, Arva Moore. *Miami: The Magic City*. Miami, FL: Centennial Press, 1991.

Polvay, Marina, and Marilyn Fellman. *Florida Heritage Cookbook*. Miami, FL: Florida Consultation and Management, 1976.

Raichlen, Steven. *Miami Spice: The New Florida Cuisine*. New York: Workman Pub, 1993.

Rawlings, Marjorie Kinnan, and Robert Camp. *Cross Creek Cookery*. New York: C. Scribner's Sons, 1942.

Sax, David. *Save the Deli: In Search of Perfect Pastrami, Crusty Rye, and the Heart of Jewish Delicatessen*. Boston: Houghton Mifflin Harcourt, 2009.

Sewell, John, and Arva Moore Parks. *Miami Memoirs*. Miami, FL: Arva Parks & Co, 1987.

Sikes, Steve. *The Holsum Story, 1913–1994: Fuchs Baking Co.* N.p., 2000.

Smiley, Nixon. *Yesterday's Miami*. Miami, FL: E.A. Seemann Pub, 1973.

Sokolov, Raymond A. *Why We Eat What We Eat: How the Encounter Between the New World and the Old Changed the Way Everyone on the Planet Eats*. New York: Summit Books, 1991.

Speir, Elizabeth, and William Schemmel. *Florida Citrus Cookbook*. Atlanta, GA: Marmac Publishing Co., 1985.

Stennis, Mary A. *Florida Fruits and Vegetables in the Commercial Menu*. Tallahassee: Florida Department of Agriculture, 1931.

Van Aken, Norman, and Janet Van Aken. *New World Kitchen: Latin American and Caribbean Cuisine*. New York: Ecco, 2003.

Van Atta, Marian. *Exotic Foods: A Kitchen and Garden Guide*. Sarasota, FL: Pineapple Press, 2002.

Villagers, Inc. *Biscayne Bights and Breezes: A Cookbook with Loving Memories of Miami*. Miami, 1987.

JOURNALS

Adams, Adam G. "Some Pre-Boom Developers of Dade County." *Tequesta* 17 (1957): 31–46.

Ammidown, Margot. "The Wagner Family: Pioneer Life on The Miami River." *Tequesta* 42 (1982): 5–38.

Andrews, Charles M. "The Florida Indians in the Seventeenth Century." *Tequesta* 3 (1943): 36–48.

Arnade, Charles W. "Cycles of Conquest in Florida." *Tequesta* 23 (1963): 23–32.

Baber, Adin. "Food Plants of the Desoto Expedition." *Tequesta* 2 (1942): 34–40.

Buchanan, Patricia. "Miami's Bootleg Boom." *Tequesta* 30 (1970): 13–31.

Burkhardt, Mrs. Henry J. "Starch Making: A Pioneer Florida Industry." *Tequesta* 12 (1952): 47–54.

Bush, Gregory W. "Anticommunism, Desegregation, and the Local News in Miami, 1945–1960." *Tequesta* 65 (2005).

Carney, James J. "Population Growth in Miami and Dade County, Florida." *Tequesta* 6 (1946): 50–55.

Chapman, Arthur. "Swedes Discover Florida." *South Florida History* (Winter 1993).

Covington, James W. "The Florida Seminoles in 1847." *Tequesta* 24 (1964): 49–58.

Davenport, Will. "Growing Up, Sort Of, in Miami, 1909–1915." *Tequesta* 40 (1980): 5–30.

Dorn, Harold W. "Mango Growing Around Early Miami." *Tequesta* 16 (1956): 37–44.

Dorn, J.K. "Recollections of Early Miami." *Tequesta* 9 (1949): 43–60.

Douthit Conrad, Mary. "Homesteading in Florida During the 1890s." *Tequesta* 17 (1957): 3–30.

Fairchild, David. "Some Plant Reminiscences of Southern Florida." *Tequesta* 2 (1942): 8–15.

Gearhardt, Earnest G., Jr. "South Florida's First Industry." *Tequesta* 12 (1952): 55–57.

George, Paul S. "Brokers, Binders, and Builders: Greater Miami's Boom of the Mid-1920s." *Florida Historical Quarterly* (July 1986).

———. "Burdines—A Century in Miami." *South Florida History* (Summer 1998).

———. "Colored Town: Miami's Black Community, 1896–1930." *Florida Historical Quarterly*, 1978.

———. "Miami and the Spanish-American War." *South Florida History* (Spring 1998).

————. "Miami's Christmastime Fire of 1896." *Florida Shipper*, February 3, 1997.

————. "The First Hundred Years." *South Florida History* (Summer 1996).

George, Paul S., and Thomas K. Peterson. "Liberty Square, 1933–1987." *Tequesta* 69 (2009).

Gifford, John C. "Five Plants Essential to the Indians and the Early Settlers of Florida." *Tequesta* 4 (1944): 36–44.

————. "Some Reflections on the Florida of Long Ago." *Tequesta* 6 (1946): 38–43.

Gilpin, Mrs. John R. "To Miami, 1890 Style." *Tequesta* 1 (1941): 89–102.

Gonzalez, Diana, and Margaret Borgeest. "Fruity Florida Recipes." *South Florida History* (Summer 1995).

Gonzalez, Diana, and Sara Maria Sanchez. "Santeria: From Africa to Miami via Cuba." *Tequesta* 48 (1998): 36–52.

Green, Henry. "Jews in Miami: South Florida's Promised Land." *South Florida History* (Fall 1998).

Graham, William A. "The Pennsuco Sugar Experiment." *Tequesta* 11 (1951): 27–50.

Hudson, F.M. "Beginnings in Dade County." *Tequesta* 3 (1943): 1–35.

Jarvis, Eric. "Foreigners from the Far North: Canadians in Miami and South Florida During the 1920s." *Tequesta* 67 (2007).

Kenward, Scott F. "Kendall and Pinecrest: Historical Antecedents of Two Communities." *Tequesta* 71 (2011).

Kleinberg, Howard. "Among the Farmers (Part 1)." *Tequesta* 48 (1988): 53–71.

————. "Among the Farmers (Part 2)." *Tequesta* 49 (1989): 69–83.

————. "Among the Farmers (Part 3)." *Tequesta* 50 (1990): 44–62.

Klose, Nelson. "Dr. Henry Perrine, Tropical Plant Enthusiast." *Florida Historical Quarterly* 27 (1948).

Leach Carson, Ruby. "Forty Years of Miami Beach." *Tequesta* 15 (1955): 3–28.

————. "Miami: 1896–1900." *Tequesta* 16 (1956): 3–14.

————. "Miami Beach Reaches the Half Century Mark." *Tequesta* 24 (1964): 3–20.

Leviten, Sara. "Jews in Miami: Isidor Cohen, the First Miami Jew." *South Florida History* (Fall 1998).

Marchman, Watt. "Florida in History and Literature." *Tequesta* 2 (1942): 63–70.

Marks, Henry S. "Earliest Land Grants in the Miami Area." *Tequesta* 18 (1958): 15–22.

Merrick, George. "Pre-Flagler Influences of the Lower Florida East Coast." *Tequesta* 1 (1941): 1–10.

Mitchell Richardson, Julie. "The Mitchells of South Dade: A Pioneer Saga." *Tequesta* 64 (2004): 50–82.

Mohl, Raymond A. "Black Immigrants: Bahamians in Early Twentieth-Century Miami." *Tequesta* 69 (2009).

————. "Interstating Miami: Urban Expressways and the Changing American City." *Tequesta* 68 (2008).

————. "Shadows in the Sunshine: Race and Ethnicity in Miami." *Tequesta* 49 (1989).

Moore Parks, Arva. "Miami in 1876." *Tequesta* 35 (1975): 89–146.

Mormino, Gary M. "Midas Returns: Miami Goes to War, 1941–1945." *Tequesta* 57 (1997): 5–51.

Munroe, Mary Barr. "Pioneer Women of Dade County." *Tequesta* 3 (1943): 49–56.

Okenfuss, Max J. "First Impressions: The Earliest Description of Florida to Circulate in Russia (1710)." *Tequesta* 30 (1970): 69–71.

Osborn, George C., and Jack P. Dalton. "Miami: From Frontier to Metropolis: An Appraisal." *Tequesta* 14 (1954): 25–50.

Perrine, Henry. "Random Records of Tropical Florida." *Tequesta* 11 (1951): 51–62.

Pozzetta, George E. "Foreign Colonies in South Florida, 1865–1910." *Tequesta* 34 (1974): 45–56.

Pozzetta, George E., and Harry A. Kersey, Jr. "Yamato Colony: A Japanese Presence in South Florida." *Tequesta* 36 (1976): 66–77.

Reed, Eve. "Funky Nights in Overtown." *South Florida History* (Spring 1993).

Robinson, T. Ralph. "Henry Perrine, Pioneer Horticulturist of Florida." *Tequesta* 2 (1942): 1–24.

Ryan, Hugh. "Tracing Miami's History Through Its Native Habitat." *South Florida History* (2007).

Sessa, Frank B. "Anti-Florida Propaganda and Countermeasures During the 1920s." *Tequesta* 21 (1961): 41–52.

———. "Miami in 1926." *Tequesta* 16 (1956): 15–36.

———. "Miami on the Eve of the Boom: 1923." *Tequesta* 11 (1951): 3–25.

Shappee, Nathan D. "Flagler's Undertakings in Miami in 1897." *Tequesta* 19 (1959): 3–14.

Smiley, Nixon. "Pioneering in Suburbia (Part 1)." *Tequesta* 50 (1990): 5–37.

Smith, Rebecca. "Fast Food in Southern Florida." *South Florida History* (Fall 1992).

Squires, Karl. "Pre-Columbian Man in Southern Florida." *Tequesta* 1 (1941): 39–46.

Staubach, James C. "Miami During the Civil War: 1861–1885." *Tequesta* 53, 1993.

Stone, Doris. "General Problems of Florida Archaeology." *Tequesta* 1 (1941): 33–38.

Straight, William M. "Early Miami through the Eyes of Youth." *Tequesta* 63 (2003): 62–77.

Sturtevant, William C. "Chakaika and the Spanish Indians." *Tequesta* 13 (1953): 35–74.

———. "A Seminole Personal Document." *Tequesta* 16 (1956): 55–75.

Todd Bingham, Millicent. "Miami: A Study in Urban Geography." *Tequesta* 8, 1948.

Wagner, Henry J. "Early Pioneers of South Florida." *Tequesta* 9 (1949): 61–72.

Welch, Jamie. "Who's Haunting Anderson's Corner?" *South Florida History* (Fall 1998).

Wiggins, Larry. "The Birth of the City of Miami." *Tequesta* 55 (1995): 5–37.

Williams, Geraldine H. "From Barbecue Shacks to the Mayfair Grill." *South Florida History* (Winter 1998).

Wilmot Voss, Kimberly. "Food Journalism or Culinary Anthropology? Re-evaluating Soft News and the Influence of Jeanne Voltz's Food Section in the *Los Angeles Times*." *American Journalism* 29, no. 2 (2012): 66–91.

Wilson, F. Page. "We Chose the Sub-Tropics." *Tequesta* 12 (1952): 19–46.

Wolff, Reinhold P. "Recent Economic Trends in South Florida." *Tequesta* 4 (1944): 45–49.

NEWSPAPER AND MAGAZINE ARTICLES

Adams, David. "'Little Buenos Aires' Booms in Miami." *St. Petersburg Times*, June 19, 2001.

Adler, Marissa. "Dogs, Fries are Arbetter's Staples." *Miami Herald*, March 24, 2002.

Albright, Mark. "An Inventory of Florida History." *Tampa Bay Times*, February 14, 2005.

Baker, Vicky. "Fusion Food in Miami." *The Guardian*, June 24, 2011.

Berggren, Helen. "Jumbo's: 51 Years of Good Food and Friends." *Miami Herald*, October 5, 2006.

Carlson, Gus. "Miami Subs to Open 110 Restaurants in Three Years." *Miami Herald*, January 10, 1992.

Chrissos, Joan. "In the '90s, a Woman's Place Is in the Kitchen." *Miami Herald*, September 25, 1997.

Cicero, Linda. "Here's News: A Funky (Not Weird) Café Eatery Adds Feel of European Bistro to South Beach." *Miami Herald*, June 27, 1989.

———. "Is This Really Cuban Food?" *Miami Herald*, August 1, 1985.

Collins, Bill. "Joe's Stone Crabs—An Annotated History." *Orlando Sentinel Star*, May 30, 1976.

Collins, Jody. "Remembering Junior's, Corky's and the Roney Pub." *Miami Herald*, January 24, 2013.

Croghan, Lore. "Miami Subs Looking to Expand Abroad." *Miami Herald*, December 21, 1992.

———. "South Florida Hotels Focusing on Food." *Miami Herald*, January 10, 1993.

Cyr, Shelby. "'Miracle Mile was the Widest Street I Had Ever Seen.'" *Miami Herald*, December 9, 2010.

Davidson, Deirdre. "Dining for Dollars Like Sand on the Beach—The South Florida Restaurant Business Shifts, Stabilizes." *Miami Herald*, August 4, 1997.

De Vosjoli, Philippe. "A Little Italy in Florida: Best Italian Restaurants." *Miami Herald*, January 13, 1978.

———. "Best Bites—15 Favorite Restaurants and Why They're Good." *Miami Herald*, December 23, 1977.

Diaz, Johnny. "Changed Beach Contributes to Demise of Gatti." *Miami Herald*, October 18, 1992.

Dunlop, Beth. "Restaurant Toasts 40 Years." *Miami Herald*, July 9, 1978.

Farmer, Lyn. "Pavilion Grill: A Downtown Treat." *Miami Herald*, June 15, 1990.

Fleischman, Joan. "Mark to Close His Place, Abandon Dade." *Miami Herald*, June 20, 1997.

Foote, Cornelius, Jr. "Chicken George Coming to Roost in Liberty City." *Miami Herald*, October 8, 1984.

George, Paul S. "Little Havana Is Modern-Day Ellis Island." *Miami Herald*, March 9, 2008.

Gersten, Alan. "Fast-Food Giants Grow, Others Falter." *Miami News*, July 28, 1975.

Grad, Molle. "Memories of Happy Times, Hearty Meals." *Miami Herald*, February 22, 2013.

Gressette, Felicia. "We Spill the Beans Faster than From-Scratch: Our Panel Finds the Top Tastes in Canned Frijoles Negros." *Miami Herald*, February 2, 1989.

Kaplan, Paul. "They Wait and Wait…and Still They're Not Crabby." *Miami News*, December 5, 1978.

Marbella, Jean. "This Is Your Bayside Guide to the Festival Marketplace." *Sun-Sentinel*, March 29, 1987.

Marquis, Christopher. "Food Fuels Nicaraguan Success Stories." *Miami Herald*, August 2, 1987.

Martin, Lydia. "Cooking Up a Neighborhood." *Miami Herald*, June 8, 2008.

McKibben, Beth. "The Real Roots of Southern Cuisine." *Deep South*, December 2012.

Miami Herald. "Dining Critic Pick S. Florida's Top 40 Eateries." February 28, 2003.

———. "The Eighties." July 21, 1996.

———. "The Fifties." July 21, 1996.

———. "The Forties." July 21, 1996.

———. "The Nineties." July 21, 1996.

———. "The Seventies." July 21, 1996.

———. "The Sixties." July 21, 1996.

———. "Visionary Restaurant Jumbo's Celebrates 50th Anniversary." January 3, 2005.

Moncreiff Arrarte, Anne. "Savoring Peru: A Hearty and Sophisticated Cuisine Emerges into the U.S. Spotlight." *Miami Herald*, March 5, 1998.

Moss, Bea. "La Choza: A Pleasing Taste of Nicaragua." *Miami Herald*, April 16, 1987.

Nordheimer, Jon. "Nicaraguan Exiles Find a Place in the Sun: Miami." *New York Times*, July 29, 1987.

Ramos, Ronnie. "Tourism Bureau Seeks New Tax." *Miami Herald*, February 1, 1989.

Reveron, Derek. "Sonic Drives Through State—Miami Men Have Aggressive Fast-food Plan." *Miami Herald*, August 9, 1991.

Rowe, Sean. "Chef Brings Old Country to New One." *Miami Herald*, October 8, 1989.

San Martin, Nancy. "Cafeteria Claims Spot atop Empanadas Heap." *Miami Herald*, June 30, 1988.

Silva, Helga. "Along Hialeah's Palm Ave.—A Changing Lifestyle at 'Mae and Dave's.'" *Miami News*, December 27, 1976.

Singer, Jill. "Landmark Eatery: Au Revoir, Mousse." *Miami Herald*, September 27, 1988.

———. "Restaurants Try to Satisfy the Kendall Appetite." *Miami Herald*, January 5, 1986.

Sommereyns, Omar. " Chef Kris Wessel Gets Back to His Roots." *Ocean Drive*, February, 2013.

Storch, Gerald. "Malls, Climate Drove out South Florida Drive-Ins." *Miami Herald*, January 15, 1978.

Tasker, Fred. "Daniel's Is a First for Dade's Gays." *Miami Herald*, January 2, 1987.

———. "Fresh Foods Have Always Been Important to South Florida Cooks." *Miami Herald*, December 26, 1999.

Tepps, David. "No Ribbing—Barbecues are Serious Business in South Dade." *Miami Herald*, August 24, 1978.

Tomb, Geoffrey. "Authentic Passage to India's Food Décor." *Miami Herald*, June 28, 1991.

———. "Bazaar Sells It All, From Wigs to Food." *Miami Herald*, June 11, 1992.

———. "The Changing Tastes of Dade Diets." *Miami Herald*, November 12, 1988.

———. "Chefs, Masters of Fish Cookery—Pacific Time Is Challenging." *Miami Herald*, August 20, 1993.

———. "Culinary Art Amid China Grill's Clamor." *Miami Herald*, November 17, 1995.

———. "Dressing Up for the Ball, Vintage 1986." *Miami Herald*, February 11, 1996.

———. "An Eggplant Grows in the Projects." *Miami Herald*, June 19, 1988.

———. "From Hula Hoops to Civil Rights: A Miami History." *Miami Herald*, May 30, 1990.

———. "The Good Life." *Miami Herald*, May 24, 1992.

———. "Grocers Open Third Store Today—Duo Is Known for Ethnic Mix." *Miami Herald*, March 3, 1991.

———. "Hometown Chef Knows Miami Tastes." *Miami Herald*, September 16, 1994.

———. "In the Beginning, 1896—Miami's Everyday Life Revealed in Detailed Diary." *Miami Herald*, April 28, 1996.

———. "Islands Have a Special Place in City's History." *Miami Herald*, June 9, 1996.

———. "Lemon City Once Lively Community Is the Town Time Forgot." *Miami Herald*, June 23, 1996.

———. "Le Pavilion's Cult of Personality Maitre D' Adds Spice to Dining Experience." *Miami Herald*, March 6, 1992.

———. "Lloyd J. Lee, Grower of Sublime South Dade Produce." *Miami Herald*, April 12, 1996.

———. "The McAllister Was City's First High-Rise Hotel." *Miami Herald*, December 3, 1987.

———. "New Culinary College Lets Students Cook Up a Career." *Miami Herald*, June 27, 1993.

———. "New Embers Stirs Old Memories." *Miami Herald*, March 3, 1995.

———. "Norma's Brings Jamaica Back to the Beach—Big, Authentic Flavor Is Well Prepared in Its Tiny Kitchen." *Miami Herald*, March 24, 1995.

———. "Once a 'Bastion of Relief,' Ice Plant Now For Sale." *Miami Herald*, July 1, 1996.

———. "Rascal House Deli Rolls into Dining's Top 50." *Miami Herald*, December 28, 1990.

———. "Something's Brewing for Miami Beer Lovers." *Miami Herald*, April 2, 1989.

———. "A Special Timepiece Marks Anniversary." *Miami Herald*, June 16, 1996.

———. "Tony Roma's New Eatery on Causeway." *Miami Herald*, March 1, 1991.

———. "What's Cooking at South Florida Restaurants?" *Miami Herald*, April 12, 1996.

———. "What's Cooking at South Florida Restaurants?" *Miami Herald*, April 19, 1996.

Varkonyi, Charlyne. "Forging a Florida Cuisine: Two South Florida Restaurants Want to Put Florida on the Culinary Map by Creating a Cuisine That Showcases All the Tasty Ingredients in the Sunshine State." *Sun-Sentinel*, September 19, 1985.

Veciana-Suarez, Ana. "Food Website Aims to be Abuela's Kitchen in Cyberspace." *Miami Herald*, August 26, 2010.

Von Maurer, Bill. "Food Stand a Dying Trade." *Miami News*, June 23, 1972.

Walker, Elaine. "Nathan's Famous to Buy Miami Subs—Companies Tout Many Synergies." *Miami Herald*, December 1, 1998.

Werne, Jo. "Design District Planners Envision World Village." *Miami Herald*, March 26, 1995.

Williams, Mike, and Chuck Strouse. "Bogus Restaurant Critic Eats and Runs." *Miami Herald*, May 7, 1989.

Wright, C.E. "Eating Is Easy at Miami Beach." *New York Times*, December 11, 1955.

WEBSITES

The Black Archives
www.theblackarchives.org

EATSFlorida
www.eatsflorida.com

Florida Department of Agriculture and Consumer Services
www.freshfromflorida.com

Florida Native Plant Society
www.fnps.org

Food Timeline
www.foodtimeline.org

Fruit and Spice Park
www.fruitandspicepark.org

HistoryMiami
www.historymiami.org

James Beard Foundation
www.jamesbeard.org

Little Havana Guide
www.littlehavanaguide.com

Miami Archives
www.miamiarchives.blogspot.com

Miami History
www.miami-history.com

My Pharmacy
www.mypharmacy.com

Slow Food Miami
www.slowfoodmiami.org

3 Guys From Miami
www.3guysfrommiami.com

Tobacco Road.
www.tobacco-road.com

Tony Roma's
www.tonyromas.com

University of Florida Institute of Food and Agricultural Sciences
http://ifas.ufl.edu/

University of Miami Digital Collections
http://scholar.library.miami.edu/miamidigital/

Versailles Restaurant
www.versaillesrestaurant.com

WLRN
www.wlrn.org

ONLINE ARTICLES AND BLOGS

Altman, Riki. "Dewey LoSasso Gets the 10—Questions, That Is." *Miami New Times* Blog, November 9, 2009. http://blogs.miaminewtimes.com/shortorder/2009/11/dewey_losasso_gets_the_10.php.

———. "Trip to Paradise Farms and Lessons in Compost." *Miami New Times* Blog, August 24, 2011. http://blogs.miaminewtimes.com/shortorder/2011/08/trip_to_paradise_farms_part_tw.php.

Anthony, Todd. "No Ordinary Joe." *Miami New Times*, May 12, 1993. http://www.miaminewtimes.com/1993-05-12/news/no-ordinary-joe/.

Brandt, Pamela Robin. "Carmen's Got It." *Miami New Times*, May 29, 2003. http://www.miaminewtimes.com/2003-05-29/restaurants/carmen-s-got-it/.

Doss, Laine. "Kris Wessel: Florida Cookery at the James Royal Palm Hotel Is Personal." *Miami New Times* Blog, September 21, 2012. http://blogs.miaminewtimes.com/shortorder/2012/09/kris_wessel_florida_cookery_is_personal.php.

Fagenson, Zachary. "Jonathan Lazar, Former Sustain Owner, Describes What Miami Lacks." *Miami New Times* Blog, November 13, 2012. http:// blogs.miaminewtimes.com/shortorder/2012/11/jonathan_lazar_ former_sustain.php.

Goyanes, Ily. "S&S Diner Proves That Not All Change Is Good." *Miami New Times* Blog, January 4, 2011. http://blogs.miaminewtimes.com/ shortorder/2011/01/ss_diner_proves_that_not_all_c.php.

Karenick, Jen. "BIG Names." *Miami New Times*, December 6, 2001. http:// www.miaminewtimes.com/2001-12-06/restaurants/big-names.

———. "Dish." *Miami New Times*, June 29, 2000. http://www. miaminewtimes.com/2000-06-29/restaurants/dish.

———. "Do the Shuffle." *Miami New Times*, May 23, 2002. http://www. miaminewtimes.com/2002-05-23/restaurants/do-the-shuffle.

———. "Generous Miami...Say What?" *Miami New Times*, January 24, 2002. http://www.miaminewtimes.com/2002-01-24/restaurants/ generous-miami-say-what.

———. "Immature Miami." *Miami New Times*, February 6, 2003. http:// www.miaminewtimes.com/2003-02-06/restaurants/immature-miami.

———. "Kerry Out." *Miami New Times*, December 15, 1993. http://www. miaminewtimes.com/1993-12-15/restaurants/kerry-out.

———. "Side Dish." *Miami New Times*, October 14, 1999. http://www. miaminewtimes.com/1999-10-14/restaurants/sidedish.

———. "Side Dish." *Miami New Times*, May 25, 2000. http://www. miaminewtimes.com/2000-05-25/restaurants/side-dish.

Katel, Jacob. "Pacific Time in the Design District Serves Cheap Eats for Recessionistas." *Miami New Times* Blog, July 8, 2009. http://blogs. miaminewtimes.com/shortorder/2009/07/pacific_time_in_the_design_ dis.php.

Klein, Lee. "Bianca at the Delano: South Beach's Bad Dining Habits Re-Emerge." *Miami New Times* Blog, April 19, 2012. http://blogs.miaminewtimes. com/shortorder/2012/04/bianca_at_the_delano_south_bea.php.

———. "The Food of Miami Cookbook." *Miami New Times* Blog, July 20, 2010. http://blogs.miaminewtimes.com/shortorder/2010/07/the_ food_of_miami.php.

———. "Miami Dining 2009: Online for a Better Future." *Miami New Times*, December 31, 2009. http://www.miaminewtimes.com/2009-12-31/restaurants/miami-dining-2009-online-for-a-better-future.

———. "Miami's Dining Scene Goes Big League." *Miami New Times*, December 25, 2008. http://www.miaminewtimes.com/2008-12-25/ restaurants/miami-s-dining-scene-enters-the-big-leagues.

———. "The 6 Best Chefs to Leave Miami." *Miami New Times* Blog, December 29, 2008. http://blogs.miaminewtimes.com/shortorder/2008/12/ the_6_best_chefs_to_leave_miam.php.

———. "South Beach Wine & Food Festival Highlight Reel." *Miami New Times*, February 25, 2010. http://www.miaminewtimes.com/2010-02-25/restaurants/south-beach-wine-food-festival-highlight-reel.

———. "Ten Best Chefs to Leave Miami Over the Past Decade." *Miami New Times* Blog, December 18, 2009. http://blogs.miaminewtimes.com/ shortorder/2009/12/ten_best_chefs_to_leave_miami.php.

———. "12 Top Miami Chefs Who Were Not Too Big to Fail, Part One." *Miami New Times* Blog, March 3, 2011. http://blogs.miaminewtimes. com/shortorder/2011/03/12_top_miami_chefs_who_were_no.php.

———. "The Year in Dining." *Miami New Times*, December 27, 2007. http://www.miaminewtimes.com/2007-12-27/restaurants/the-year-in-dining.

———. "What's the Matter with Miami?" *Miami New Times*, November 24, 2005. http://www.miaminewtimes.com/2005-11-24/restaurants/what-s-the-matter-with-miami/full.

Leite, David. "Dining through the Decades: 100 Years of American Food." Leite's Culinaria. http://leitesculinaria.com/10348/writings-dining-through-the-decades-american-food-history.html.

McCart, Melissa. "Women Chefs Struggle to Break into Fine Dining's Good Ol' Boys Club." *Miami New Times*, February 2, 2012. http://www.miaminewtimes.com/2012-02-02/restaurants/women-chefs-struggle-to-break-into-fine-dining-s-good-ol-boys-club.

Powers, Jacquelynn D. "The Real Reason Top Chef's Micah Edelstein Left Grass." *Miami New Times* Blog, May 11, 2010. http://blogs.miaminewtimes.com/shortorder/2010/05/the_real_reason_top_chefs_mica.php.

Semple, Kirk. "Dade's Greatest Hits." *Miami New Times*, July 27, 1995. http://www.miaminewtimes.com/1995-07-27/news/dade-s-greatest-hits.

———. "55 SW Miami Avenue Road." *Miami New Times*, December 5, 1996. http://www.miaminewtimes.com/1996-12-05/news/55-sw-miami-avenue-road.

———. "Mano a Mano." *Miami New Times*, May 19, 1993. http://www.miaminewtimes.com/1993-05-19/news/mano-a-mano.

INDEX

A

Allapattah 24, 36

B

Baker, Charles, Jr. 57
Bayside Marketplace 84
Biltmore Hotel 48
Brownsville 60
Burdine's 21, 49
Burger King 104

C

Civil War 33
Coconut Grove 24, 34, 36, 46, 47, 57,
    77, 83
coontie 14, 18, 19, 35

D

Dadeland 21, 77
delis 7, 8, 73, 74, 89, 133

E

East Coast Fisheries 52
Eden Roc 70, 72

Eighteen-Day Reducing Diet 62
English, William 33

F

Fitzpatrick, Richard 33
Flagler, Henry 33, 35, 38, 54
Fontainebleau 70, 72, 119
food blogs 93
Forge, The 52, 53

G

Galatis, Jerry 38
Gatti's Restaurant 59
Great Depression 47, 49, 58, 59
Great Gables, The 67, 74

H

Holsum Bakery 106

J

Jamaica Inn 69
James Beard Foundation Awards 88, 93,
    94
Joe's Stone Crab 45, 52, 97

K

Kendall 23, 83, 133

L

Lemon City 36, 47, 99, 102, 132
lionfish 18
Little Haiti 24, 28, 36, 83
Little Havana 24, 28, 75, 83, 84, 128

M

Mango Gang 78, 84, 86, 87, 88, 89, 92,
    127, 128
Marcus, Joshua 74, 89
McAllister Hotel 41
McArthur Dairy 100
Miami Beach 9, 41, 45, 48, 50, 56, 73,
    74, 77, 83, 88, 92, 119, 132, 142
Miami Subs Grill 106
Mutiny Hotel 84

O

oranges 11, 13, 15, 17, 32, 35, 36, 68
Overtown 24, 37, 38, 60, 70, 75

P

Peacock Inn 34
Pollo Tropical 104
Prohibition 45, 48, 54, 55, 56, 57
    Nation, Carrie 55
Publix 101, 102

R

recipes
    Arrowroot Drop Cakes 20
    Bananas with Cheese 120
    Bear Steak 110
    Carissa Cream 112
    Cheese and Green Pea Salad 121
    Chicken Coconut Grove 114
    Cocoanut Pudding 118
    Deviled Dip 111
    Dried Beef Dip 115
    Ember's Famous French Dressing 68
    Florida Dessert Salad 66

Florida Fruit Special 66
Florida Green Ice Cream 119
Florida Pecan Sandwiches 122
Florida Sunshine Salad 116
Guava Pudding 118
Jellied Tongue 109
JFK Salad Dressing 119
Mayhaw Jelly 110
Noodle Croquettes 116
Piave Salad 108
Pineapple-Cheese Salad 111
Roselle Jam 121
Sea Foam 108
suckling pig 58
Tropical Catsup 120
Turkey Barbecue with Avocado 112
Turtle Steaks 115
Regal Beer 53
ribs 80
Royal Castle 8, 104
Royal Palm Hotel 39

S

Schwartz, Michael 87, 88, 89, 91, 96
Sedano's 101, 104
Sheba Ethiopian Restaurant 91, 128

T

Tequesta Indians 13, 24, 29, 32, 33, 34
The Seven Seas Restaurant and Marine
    Cocktail Lounge 38, 50
Tobacco Road 45
Tuttle, Julia 33, 35, 38, 39, 54

U

Urbanite Bistro 91

W

Waters, Alice 78, 84, 86
Wessel, Kris 87, 92, 133, 135
Winn-Dixie 101, 102
Wo Kee & Son Co. 48